Secular City, Sacred Soul

Spirituality and Society

Secular City, Sacred Soul

GRAHAM JOSEPH HILL

Eagna Publishing • Sydney, Australia

SECULAR CITY, SACRED SOUL

Published by: Eagna Publishing (Sydney, Australia)
eagnapublishing@icloud.com
Cover and interior design: Graham Joseph Hill
www.grahamjosephhill.com

paperback isbn: 978-1-7641791-6-4
ebook isbn: 978-1-7641791-7-1
version number: 2025-11-12

NATIONAL LIBRARY OF AUSTRALIA

A catalogue record for this book is available from the National Library of Australia

Contents

Introduction: Finding God in the Secular City

The city hums. The city brings delights and pains. Beneath the sound of traffic and commerce, beneath the laughter in laneways and the ache behind apartment walls, something holy emerges. There's a heartbeat under the asphalt and in the concrete and skyscrapers: a presence that the city's noise and busyness can't silence. The Spirit of God still walks these streets. Yet few stop long enough to notice.

We live in an age of noise and velocity. Our calendars are full, our attention fractured, our souls stretched thin. The world moves faster than our capacity for meaning. Our hands scroll while our hearts sleep. We mistake motion for life, noise for community, performance for meaning, and visibility for worth. In this restless secular age, faith can feel like a foreign language: an echo from another time, faintly remembered and easily dismissed. And yet, even here, God waits.

This book offers insights for those who suspect that the sacred still pulses beneath the secular, that the city itself may yet become an environment of God's divine presence. It's written for those who sense that faith must learn a new language: not of triumph but of tenderness, not of conquest but of compassion, not of escape but of encounter. *Secular City, Sacred Soul* belongs to the *Spirituality and Society* series, which explores how the way of Jesus shapes our inner life and calls us into courageous engagement with the world. These reflections were first shared with readers of my Substack, *Spirituality and Society with Hilly*, and they're gathered here as a single conversation: a prayerful attempt to hear what the Spirit is saying to the churches amid the noise of modern life.

1

The Desert Within the City

Ours isn't the first culture to wrestle with spiritual barrenness. The prophets knew what it meant to live among ruins and still speak of hope. Ezekiel stood in a valley of dry bones and asked, *Can these bones live?* Isaiah cried out to a people drunk on idols and injustice, calling them back to the water of life. Jesus walked through Jerusalem's crowded markets and declared that the kingdom of God was among them: hidden, small, yet unstoppable. The same Spirit that brooded over creation now broods over our cities, over their wounds and wonders, over their violence and yearning.

We're witnessing a great unraveling. Churches shrink; trust fractures; meaning thins. The gods of our age (consumerism, nationalism, individualism, and algorithmic distraction) promise abundance but deliver exhaustion. We worship productivity while neglecting presence. We build towers of progress and forget people experiencing poverty who sweep the floors beneath them. We curate perfect digital lives while loneliness metastasizes. The West, once drunk on religious certainty, now stumbles through a long night of forgetfulness.

But what if this isn't death? What if it's a descent? The mystics remind us that divine love sometimes withdraws its consolations, not to punish but to purify: to teach us to love God for God's sake, and not for comfort or control. Perhaps the secular age is our own dark night, stripping away the false gods that once propped up our faith. Perhaps this unraveling is grace in disguise: a refining fire burning away triumphalism, nationalism, and nostalgia, so that something truer might emerge: a humbler, quieter, more merciful Christianity.

Contemplatives in the Crowd

If the desert fathers sought God in solitude, our monastery is now the metro, the marketplace, the glowing screen. The contemplative life no longer hides behind monastery walls; it must learn to dwell among the crowd without losing its center. The call of Jesus hasn't changed; only the landscape has. "Follow me," he still says, not into withdrawal but into deeper presence.

To follow him now is to cultivate attention in a culture that monetizes distraction. It's to pray with eyes open in a world that prefers sleep. It's to carry silence like a lamp through streets humming with noise. The contemplative doesn't escape the city; they bless it. They find God not despite the chaos but within it: in the glimmer of compassion between strangers, in the courage of truth-telling, in the quiet dignity of those who refuse to give up on love.

But contemplation alone isn't enough. Prayer without justice is sentimentality; justice without prayer is self-righteousness. The prophets and the mystics belong together. Moses ascends the mountain to meet God, but he descends again to confront Pharaoh. Elijah hears God in silence, then speaks fire into corruption. Mary of Nazareth ponders divine mystery in her heart, then sings revolution into being: "He has brought down the mighty and lifted up the lowly."

So must we. The contemplative life must give birth to the prophetic life. Silence must give rise to speech, prayer to protest, stillness to solidarity.

The Idols We Serve

Every age has its idols. Ours are sophisticated, digital, and respectable. They're often referred to by names such as growth, security, productivity, and identity. They promise control but deliver captivity. The god of nationalism offers belonging through exclusion. The god of consumerism promises freedom through possession. The god of technology promises omniscience but robs us of wonder. The god of certainty promises safety but crucifies mystery.

These idols thrive on fear: fear of scarcity, of insignificance, of the other. But fear is the enemy of faith. The God of Jesus Christ doesn't secure power through domination but through self-emptying love. At the

3

cross, God exposes the futility of our idols. At the resurrection, God unveils a new creation: one born not of conquest but of communion.

If we're to follow Christ in this secular age, we must unmask these idols in ourselves and in our systems. We must learn again what it means to be human: creatures of dust and glory, finite yet beloved, stewards rather than masters. The city won't be saved by efficiency, but by empathy; not by walls, but by tables; not by algorithms, but by the grace that moves unseen through ordinary lives; not by false gods, but by the crucified and risen Christ.

Hope in the Ruins

There are ruins everywhere: moral, ecological, relational, spiritual. Yet Scripture insists that resurrection begins in ruins. The risen Christ did not appear in palaces or parliaments but in gardens, kitchens, and locked rooms. He met women who wept, doubters who feared, disciples who hid. His body still bore wounds. Resurrection isn't the erasure of suffering but its transformation.

Our hope, then, isn't that the world will return to what it was, but that grace will rise where it's least expected. I see resurrection in refugee communities planting gardens in bombed-out soil. I see it in churches feeding the hungry without asking for credentials. I see it in artists who still dare to paint beauty in a cynical age, and in young activists who fight for justice not because they're naive but because they still believe love has the final word.

This is the hope that sustains us: not optimism, but resurrection faith: the stubborn conviction that even in death, God is at work bringing life. The gospel isn't escapism; it's engagement. It calls us to rebuild from the ruins, to plant vineyards in the wasteland, to sing alleluia with dirt still under our nails.

The Invitation

Secular City, Sacred Soul isn't a manual or manifesto. It's a pilgrimage in words: a series of reflections born from prayer, pain, and longing. Each chapter began as a meditation shared on my Substack, *Spirituality and Society with Hilly*, written for readers hungry for depth in a shallow time. These pages have been integrated as one sustained invitation: to practice presence in a distracted age, to recover the contemplative heart of discipleship, and to live with cruciform hope in a world that forgets God but can't escape grace.

This book moves in three parts. The first listens to the ache of our secular age: its loneliness, forgetfulness, and distraction. The second explores pathways of discernment: how contemplation and compassion, silence and speech, mystery and justice might meet. The third turns to the cross and resurrection, where love's most profound truth is revealed: that God isn't absent from our suffering but present within it, and that from death, something wholly new can rise.

The invitation is simple, though never easy: to live as contemplatives in the crowd and prophets in the city. To pray in traffic. To love across divides. To listen for God in the noise. To see holiness shimmering through the ordinary.

The kingdom of God isn't elsewhere. It's here: in the subway and the marketplace, the office and the alley, the laughter of children and the silence between sirens. God isn't waiting for a more spiritual age. God is here, now, longing to be known.

So, pause. Breathe. Look again. The ground beneath your feet is holy. The city isn't godless; it's only distracted. And the Spirit still hovers: brooding over chaos, whispering over water, calling forth life.

The question isn't whether God is present.

The question is: *Will we notice?*

PART I — THE SOUL IN A SECULAR AGE: DIAGNOSIS AND LONGING

Part 1 explores the cultural and spiritual disorientation of contemporary secular societies: our loneliness, distraction, and forgetfulness of God.

1. Secular City, Sacred Soul: Finding God in a Post-Christian Urban Jungle

The city hums with restlessness. Sirens, construction, and conversation coil around one another in a relentless liturgy of noise, desire, and urgency. In these concrete cathedrals of commerce, image, movement, and ambition, the soul often seems like an afterthought, something left behind in the commute or buried beneath the algorithm.

Faith, in the modern city, can feel like a foreign dialect, a strange orientation, a useless past-time, a bygone superstition. And yet, urban spirituality is precisely the place where the presence of God moves unseen, waiting not in escape but encounter, emerging not in retreat but in the sacred presence of Christ manifesting in the ordinary life of the city.

Practicing Presence in a Distracted Age

God isn't absent in the urban jungle. But to find God here requires a new kind of seeing, a contemplative attentiveness that doesn't flee the city's chaos but finds stillness within it. The call isn't to abandon the marketplace but to become monks of the metro, saints of the sidewalk, and contemplatives in the crowd.

"The soul doesn't need a monastery to find God; it needs attention."

The holy isn't hidden from the secular world; it's woven through it, waiting to be touched, named, and received. Anyone who says God's holy and beautiful presence isn't found in the mess, chaos, noise, and people of cities hasn't been looking closely enough or paying attention to God.

This is where the old wisdom of practicing presence becomes urgent and subversive.[1] The soul doesn't need a monastery to find God; it needs attention. Urban spirituality requires a willingness to wake up, notice, and pray with eyes open in a world that wants them closed. The question isn't whether God is present in secular spaces but whether we are.

The Spiritual Crisis of Forgetfulness

Many who dwell in cities now live without the scaffolding of institutional religion, communal worship, natural landscapes, silent retreat, or sacred rhythm. The economic calendar has replaced the sacred one. Sunday mornings are market or brunch time, and meaning is often shaped more by Netflix and newsfeeds than by Scripture, liturgy, or silence.

"The spiritual crisis of the city isn't its secularity; it's its forgetfulness."

But the soul still hungers. Beneath the noise, people long for transcendence, rootedness, and peace that doesn't come in a bottle or through a screen. The spiritual crisis of the city isn't its secularity; it's its forgetfulness. The Spirit is reaching out to hearts with love and grace, wanting people to remember their belovedness, sacredness, and connectedness to Someone larger than themselves, bigger than their fears and anxieties, more significant than their ambitions and desires, and grander than their skyscrapers and cities.

Finding Burning Bushes in the Digital Glow

In every city, the Spirit hovers above the concrete and steel, within the humanity and connections, bringing God's shalom and redemption. Among the steel and digital glow are burning bushes, small moments of grace present in the ordinary.[2]

---

[1] Brother Lawrence, *The Practice of the Presence of God.*
[2] Taylor, *An Altar in the World.*

"The city isn't godless; it's often just distracted."

God's grace breaks through as light filters through a train window; a stranger shows kindness on a crowded street or an unnoticed sparrow flitters across the pavement. These are sacraments, too. The city isn't godless; it's often just distracted.

We usually don't find God in dramatic visions or spiritual highs but in the simple act of presence: washing dishes, sweeping floors, changing nappies, commuting to work, paying bills, smiling at strangers, riding elevators, and answering emails. In all these things and more, God is near. Practicing God's presence means letting no moment be wasted, no space be too secular, and no task be too mundane to become a communion site.[3]

Altars on the Move

Jesus knew this. He taught on dusty roads, healed in marketplaces, prayed in lonely places, and wept outside the gates of cities. His ministry unfolded in the middle of human noise and need. Jesus noticed fig trees, fields, coins, lepers, sparrows, lilies, and children.[4] He moved slowly through crowds and saw what others ignored. His spirituality was of deep presence, not detachment, a grounded way of being that saw through surfaces into the sacred center of things.

"The subway becomes a monastery, the café a cathedral, the workplace a chapel, and the park bench a prayer stool."

To follow Jesus in the city isn't to withdraw but to embody this same attentive love. The subway becomes a monastery, the café a cathedral, the workplace a chapel, and the park bench a prayer stool. We carry the inner room of stillness within us, even when the world spins

---

3 Brother Lawrence, *The Practice of the Presence of God*; Taylor, *A Secular Age*.
4 See, for example, Matthew 6:26–30; Luke 12:24–27; Luke 15:8–10; Mark 11:13; Nouwen, *Making All Things New*.

fast around us. We become altars on the move, bearing grace in brief encounters, silent prayers, and small, intentional acts of love.

Of course, this takes practice. The soul must be trained to resist the tyranny of speed and spectacle. It must learn to breathe, listen, and be still, not in escape but in the heart of motion. Without such formation, the city will shape us in its image: restless, reactive, fragmented, distracted, always searching, and never arriving.

But if we choose differently, if we surrender not to the noise but to love, we may find the sacred hidden in plain sight: in laughter shared between strangers, in the quiet dignity of work done well, in beauty glimpsed between buildings, in arms outstretched toward immigrants, in prayer whispered between meetings, in lament offered while walking through injustice, and in the quiet assurance that we aren't alone, even when no one sees us.

"The world doesn't need more escape. It needs presence: deep, rooted, alert presence."

The secular city may not speak the language of church bells, choirs, and incense, but it isn't beyond the reach of God. Every pavement and platform can become holy ground. And the soul, even here, even now, can burn with sacred fire.

The world doesn't need more escape. It needs presence: deep, rooted, alert presence. The kind that listens in traffic, prays over spreadsheets, and welcomes grace into every square inch of urban life. The kingdom of God isn't elsewhere. It's here.

"Jesus Christ still walks the streets. Will we walk with him?"

God's loving presence is often hidden in noise, buried in busyness, and reaching out to us as we wait in line at the bank or post office. The Spirit of Christ longs to touch our hearts, reassuring us of our belovedness on subways, streets, office towers, and city parks. And Jesus

Christ still walks the streets. Will we walk with him?[5] Will we see God in our cities?

[5] Hunter, *To Change the World.*

2. The Decline of Religion or the Dark Night of the West?

Something's shifting in the West's soul. Churches sit emptier. Familiar creeds fade from memory. Statues are toppled, not just from public squares but from the heart's inner sanctum. Many look around and wonder: Is this the end of faith in the modern world? Has religion run its course in Western culture, a relic of the past fading into the digital dusk?

"What if this isn't a death? What if it's a descent? Not into despair, but into something deeper."

But what if this isn't a death? What if it's a descent? Not into despair, but into something deeper. The old mystics knew a strange truth: the soul sometimes must pass through a night so dark that it feels like abandonment.[6] Yet that very darkness is where something luminous begins. What if the spiritual unraveling we see around us isn't collapse but a kind of purification? What if the West isn't faithless but being led through its own "dark night"?

The Dark Night as a Map, Not a Mourning

John of the Cross spoke of the "dark night of the soul" not as punishment but as purgation: a painful grace.[7] In infinite tenderness, God sometimes withdraws the consolations of felt presence. Having grown too dependent on spiritual sweetness or certainty, the soul learns

---

[6] John of the Cross, *The Dark Night of the Soul.*
[7] John of the Cross, *The Dark Night of the Soul.*

to love God for God's sake instead. In the absence of light, we discover what our love is made of.

Now consider the Western world. We once lived in what felt like a spiritually saturated culture: church bells marking time, religious holidays shaping calendars, and faith stitched into the fabric of daily life. But that familiarity often became institutional, assumed, even rote. The structures remained, but the fire dimmed. And maybe now, the scaffolding is falling away, so something more essential can emerge.

The decline of religion may be less about loss and more about refining. It's uncomfortable, even excruciating. But the night isn't abandonment. It's an invitation.

"The decline of religion may be less about loss and more about refining. It's uncomfortable, even excruciating. But the night isn't abandonment. It's an invitation."

When God Feels Absent: The Cultural Echo

In a dark night, the soul feels like God's gone silent. Prayer dries up. Scripture sounds hollow. The warmth of previous seasons fades. For many, this can feel like failure or divine rejection. But for the mystics, it's a deepening: a pulling back so the soul might grow in longing, trust, and purity.

Isn't this what we see in much of Western secularism? A felt absence. A spiritual silence. People report longing for meaning, yearning for transcendence, yet turning away from inherited forms of faith. Many raised in religious homes describe feeling as if the presence they once knew has vanished. They've walked away not because they're indifferent but because what once nourished now feels hollow.

"Maybe this cultural malaise isn't faithlessness but thirst. Perhaps it's not the denial of God but disorientation in God's apparent silence."

13

Maybe this cultural malaise isn't faithlessness but thirst. Perhaps it's not the denial of God but disorientation in God's apparent silence. The West isn't alone in this experience. It's walking a path the mystics charted long ago: a painful purgation that strips away false images, leaving the soul naked and true.

Stripped Down to Longing

The dark night empties the soul of idols, not just golden calves but subtler ones: certainty, security, reputation, power, and control. It teaches us to relinquish our expectations of God, our need to feel "spiritual," and our addiction to inspiration. What's left is a raw, wordless longing and hunger we can't name but also can't shake.

Isn't this the mood and yearning that lingers beneath the surface of our time? Beneath the noise of culture wars and the rise of the "nones" is a deep spiritual homesickness. Many are done with religion but not with the sacred.[8] They're tired of formulas but still listening for divine presence. The yearning hasn't died; it's been refined.

The night reveals what we truly hunger for: not a nostalgic return to Christendom but a lived encounter with the Holy, not a new program or polished answer but presence, mystery, and depth.

The Cross as Companion

For the mystics, the dark night isn't traversed alone. It's walked with the Crucified One. Christ doesn't watch us wander from a distance. Christ descends with us into the shadows.

"The night reveals what we truly hunger for: not a nostalgic return to Christendom but a lived encounter with the Holy, not a new program or polished answer but presence, mystery, and depth."

This is no easy comfort. It's not the promise of a quick exit or restored familiarity. It's the assurance that even in obscurity, we're not

---

[8] Taylor, *A Secular Age.*

forsaken. The One who cried out in abandonment on the cross understands this silence. And through that silence, something new was born.

Western spirituality may be undergoing a similar cruciform transformation. As public religion fades, as churches lose their place of privilege, something hidden might be forming: a kinder, humbler, more honest faith that doesn't seek dominance but presence, not performance but love.[9]

A Hidden Renewal

What if we're witnessing not the decline of Christianity but its transformation? Not its erasure, but its simplification? There's beauty in things being pared down to their essence. Many are rediscovering ancient practices: contemplation, silence, lament, hospitality. They're lighting candles in small rooms, praying alone on subway rides, seeking God in the margins.

The renewal may not look like revival tents or massive movements. It may look like seeds in the dirt, like tears in the night. But it's real. And it's rising.

This is how spiritual life often moves: not with fanfare, but with fermentation. Beneath the apparent decay, the soil is being turned. Something new is being made ready.

Hope in the Night

So, we need not fear the dark. It's not the absence of God but the refining of our sight. It's not death but gestation. The Western soul may be aching and disoriented, but hasn't been abandoned. It's being gently led into mystery.

The question isn't how we recover cultural dominance or rebuild lost institutions. The question is: How do we remain faithful in the dark?

---

[9] Hunter, *To Change the World.*

How do we listen when there's no sound? How do we trust when the path disappears?

Faithfulness in the night means letting go of what no longer gives life, practicing unseen acts of love, turning toward God even when God feels absent, and waiting with hope, even when there's no guarantee of dawn.

Dawn Comes Softly

Every dark night has a purpose. And every dark night gives way to morning. Not always the morning we imagined, but one shaped by grace.

The West may never return to its old religious forms. But maybe it isn't meant to. Maybe something truer is emerging: less showy, more surrendered. Less certainty, more trust. Less control, more love.

The invitation is to walk this night with open hands. To trust that even in silence, the Holy is near. To believe that what looks like loss may be clearing space for something more profound than we've ever known.

"The dark night isn't the end. It's the place where dawn begins."

3. Lonely But Not Alone: Contemplative Responses to the Loneliness Epidemic

We live side by side, screen to screen, yet something hurts in our souls. The world's more connected than ever, with instant messages, always-on feeds, and endless social media updates. Still, the soul feels strangely unheld. Loneliness doesn't just visit the elderly or the marginalized. It walks beside students in crowded lecture halls, professionals in packed elevators, parents at playgrounds, marriages and intimate relationships, and pastors and parishioners in full sanctuaries. There's an epidemic under the noise: a widespread yearning to be seen, known, and loved. Does anyone see me? Am I valued and loved? Would I be missed if I wasn't here? And in this crisis of connection, spiritual voices from centuries past offer unexpected guidance: you might be lonely, but you're not alone.

What if solitude isn't our enemy but a doorway? What if ancient wisdom, carried by desert monks and contemplative mystics, could guide us through the fog of isolation into a deeper, healing presence? The call of contemplation isn't to escape loneliness by filling our lives with more noise, people, or activity. It's to meet loneliness honestly and there, to discover a sacred presence that doesn't abandon, even in the silence. God reaches out to our hearts in our loneliness and offers intimacy and comfort amid our heartache and suffering.

The Difference Between Loneliness and Solitude

Loneliness is the feeling, and often the pain, of disconnection. It's what we feel when our desire for closeness goes unmet and when we sense we're invisible or unnecessary. It's not just being alone: it's feeling abandoned, emotionally stranded in a crowded world. And loneliness is everywhere. Surveys show rising levels of isolation and mental health distress in nearly every age group and social setting. Something's gone missing in our shared life: presence, depth, connection, warmth, and care.

But solitude is different. Solitude isn't the absence of people; it's the presence of God. It's the sacred space where we learn to be at home with ourselves and the One who created us. In solitude, we're not escaping connection; we're deepening it. The early desert and contemplative Christians understood this.[10] They left behind cities not out of contempt for people but to strip away distractions and encounter God without filters. They believed the desert, wilderness, or secret place wasn't empty but full of voices, struggles, angels, creation, belovedness, and most of all, divine presence. They faced their inner chaos not to be consumed by it but to be transformed within it.

"Solitude isn't the absence of people; it's the presence of God."

Contemplative solitude invites us into that same journey. It doesn't pretend away the pain of loneliness. It meets it with radical honesty, then gently holds it until something sacred emerges. The invitation isn't to deny our longing for connection but to bring it into prayer and God's presence. Solitude becomes not a sentence but a sanctuary.

When Loneliness Lingers

Not all loneliness is fleeting. For some, it lingers like fog, stubborn and unseen. There are those whose loneliness is wrapped in loss: a partner buried, a child estranged, a friendship vanished. Others live on the margins, made invisible by age, illness, disability, race, or difference.

---

[10] Merton, *The Wisdom of the Desert.*

Some wake each morning to silence and aloneness not by choice but by circumstance, and the ache isn't a doorway but a daily companion.

This kind of loneliness (chronic, complex, sometimes unnamed) asks for deeper compassion. It doesn't always yield quickly to spiritual practice. And that's okay. God isn't impatient. God is particularly tender in those places where others pass by too quickly.

In the Gospels, Jesus sought out the lonely: the woman at the well, the bleeding woman, the forgotten leper, and the tax collector up in a tree.[11] Each bore a kind of loneliness the world didn't know how to hold. But Jesus did. And still does.

If your loneliness feels unfixable, you're not doing anything wrong. This isn't about trying harder. It's about letting yourself be seen. Even here (especially here) the Spirit says to your heart, "I'm with you." The fog doesn't lift all at once. But you're not walking through it alone.

What the Desert Taught the Soul

The Desert Fathers and Mothers left us a strange kind of map. Their wisdom is untamed and peculiar. Their stories are filled with silence, sweat, wanderings, seclusion, visions, and wrestling. They embraced solitude not as a spiritual flex but as a path toward communion. Alone in the wilderness, they confronted their fears, their illusions, and their hungers. These contemplatives found a deeper spring in the very place of barrenness.

Abba Moses once said, "Sit in your cell, and your cell will teach you everything."[12] (By "cell," he means a prayer corner, inner room, personal retreat space, or spiritual hideaway). Abba Moses wasn't prescribing isolation for its own sake. He described a kind of spiritual listening: staying put long enough for the heart to settle, the ego to soften, the desire for God to grow, and the still small voice to emerge. In that quiet space, not immediately but over time, they discovered they

---

11 Luke 19:1–10; John 4:1–26; Luke 5:12–16. These passages illustrate Jesus's ministry to the lonely, sick, and marginalized.
12 Ward, trans., *The Sayings of the Desert Fathers.*

weren't alone at all. God was there. Always had been. But it took solitude to learn how to see.

We don't need to flee into the desert or wilderness to learn this. Our contemporary monastery can be the metro, subway, living room, library, university campus, office lunchroom, or corner of a city park. What matters isn't the setting but the posture. Contemplative solitude is a choice to stop running, breathe deeply, face our interior life with compassion and curiosity, and trust that God will meet us there.

Practices That Transform Loneliness into Prayer

How do we enter solitude in a world that prizes noise and motion? How do we move from painful isolation to sacred presence? Here are a few spiritual practices that can help:

1. Breath Prayer

Choose a simple phrase, something like "God, you're here," "Jesus, you're close," or "I am held in love." Repeat it slowly with your breath. Inhale the first part, exhale the second. Let it sink into your body, deep into your heart, not just your mind. When loneliness rises, return to the breath. This prayer doesn't fix the ache but anchors you in something deeper than feeling.

2. Silence with God

Set a timer for five or ten minutes. Sit in stillness. No need to perform or speak. Let your loneliness be present. Don't push it away. Imagine sitting beside Christ, saying nothing, just being together. You don't need to impress or improve. Just be. In the silence, let your ache become a prayer. Let it speak without words.

"The silence isn't empty. It's full."

3. The Examen of Longing

At the end of the day, take five minutes to name what you longed for most.[13] Was it attention? Touch? Belonging? Affection? To be seen? Rest? Offer those longings to God. Ask, gently, where they pointed. Sometimes, our loneliness is the compass needle of the soul, pointing to where love wants to meet us.

4. Sacred Listening

Reach out to someone you trust. Ask for a listening ear and offer the same. But don't rush to fix or give advice. Just practice being with one another. Contemplative solitude teaches us how to be present to ourselves: from that, we can offer a deeper presence to others. Solitude strengthens community, not the other way around.

5. Touch Creation

The natural world is a companion. A tree doesn't need you to be impressive. A river doesn't rush you along. A beach doesn't ask you to produce. Take a walk. Sit under the sky. Swim in the ocean. Let the earth remind you of something enduring and generous. Even in the heart of a city, the sacred still grows in soil and sky.

From Isolation to Intimacy

Loneliness can feel like exile. But in the language of the Spirit, exile is often the beginning of encounter, belonging, and formation of a new identity. The ache of absence can become the womb of intimacy. It takes courage to sit with that pain, to stop numbing, and to start listening. But if we stay with it (with open hands and a soft heart) we'll find that our God hasn't abandoned us. Instead, God's Spirit invites us into a deeper and more holistic kind of knowing.

"The ache of absence can become the womb of intimacy."

---

[13] The Examen is an Ignatian spiritual practice. See: Ignatius of Loyola, *The Spiritual Exercises of Saint Ignatius.*

Contemplative solitude doesn't erase our need for people. It simply makes our relationships more honest. When we learn to be at home in ourselves with God, we bring less desperation into our connections. We have become less needy and more present, less frantic, and freer. Loneliness softens. And slowly, solitude becomes a friend.

"Contemplative solitude doesn't erase our need for people. It simply makes our relationships more honest."

You're Not Alone

Louder media or bigger gatherings won't solve the loneliness epidemic. It calls for something quieter, deeper, slower. This epidemic asks us to rediscover presence: with ourselves, with God, with creation, and with each other. The monastics knew this. Jesus knew this. And we can learn it too.

You might be lonely. But you're not alone.

Right now, in this breath, the Spirit is near. The silence isn't empty. It's full. And the God who dwells in lonely, quiet places also dwells in you. You're seen. You're held. You're precious. You're loved. And even here, even now, you are being gently invited home: into God's loving care and presence.

"You might be lonely. But you're not alone."

4. Doomscrolling and Pseudo-Transcendence

Doomscrolling is the habit of endlessly scrolling through negative news or distressing social media content, especially during times of crisis or uncertainty.[14] It's the compulsive consumption of bad news (natural disasters, political unrest, global pandemics, social collapse) often late at night or in moments of anxiety. It feels like staying informed, but it's frequently driven by fear, helplessness, or a subconscious craving for control.[15] Doomscrolling is digital overexposure to crisis without stillness, prayer, or discernment. It's a habit of looking that forms us, often away from love, presence, and peace.

Doomscrolling is a liturgy in disguise, a ritual of staring into glowing rectangles, searching not for beauty or truth but for some glimmer of control amidst the chaos.[16] It feels like focus, like paying attention, but beneath the surface, it hollows the soul. It promises knowing but delivers numbness. What happens when the act of watching becomes a substitute for the act of praying? How are our souls shaped by the practice of constantly scrolling for information, stimulation, validation, and connection?

There's space for presence, encounter, and prayer in the silence we avoid. But silence has become unbearable. The crisis is more

---

[14] This definition and concept were first popularized during the COVID-19 pandemic. Jennings Brown, "How 'Doomscrolling' Can Be Addictive."
[15] This idea is supported by research into compulsive media consumption and its psychological roots. See Schroder and Wertz, "COVID-19 and Doomscrolling."
[16] This metaphor echoes themes from Smith, particularly his argument that cultural habits form the soul like liturgies. See Smith, *You Are What You Love*.

comfortable than stillness, outrage more familiar than peace, noise more common than silence, and bad news more attention-grabbing than the good news of the gospel of Jesus Christ.[17] We scroll not because we're curious but because we're lonely, anxious, afraid, and addicted. These feeds become temples of false transcendence, where meaning is manufactured, not received. For many people today, searching for news replaces searching for wisdom.

This restless seeking reveals a deeper ache for intimacy, transcendence, grounding, and belonging. Our fingers flick the screen, but our hearts long to touch eternity. The world is chaotic and in crisis, but our souls long for the peace and reassurance of God.

Why do we keep returning to what leaves us more anxious than before? Since the Garden of Eden, humans have traded the peace, love, and security of God's shalom and presence for the noise, conflict, and anxiety of our egos, ambitions, distractions, rebellions, and distorted desires. The problem is ancient. The solution remains the same. Our only hope is God.

We become what we behold. The gaze forms the soul.[18] If we feed our eyes on disruption, our hearts will mirror the noise. Doomscrolling forms anxious, reactive souls rather than grounded ones. What might it mean to reclaim attention as an act of love, not compulsion?

---

[17] This reflection resonates with insights into media design and the attention economy, particularly regarding how outrage and novelty are incentivized online. See Newport, *Digital Minimalism.*
[18] The idea that beholding shapes being is a theme developed across Christian spiritual formation literature. See *The Way of the Heart* by Nouwen, especially in his reflections on solitude and attention.

5. TikTok, Temptations, and Teresa's Interior Castle

We scroll for comfort. We swipe for connection. We post, react, and refresh, yet we still feel hollow. The endless feed promises escape but rarely delivers rest. It lures with novelty and leaves the soul weary. Christians today aren't just fighting sin; they're drowning in noise.

But the noise is more than an inconvenience: it can be a spiritual warfare of subtle temptations, pulling us from the love of God and neighbor, and dulling our desire for holiness. The temptations are subtle, often not immoral but numbing, including hours lost to distraction, attention fragmented, and identity shaped more by likes than love. The enemy in this age doesn't come roaring, although it's undoubtedly prowling. This adversary arrives in the soft hum of passive scrolling, the slow erosion of stillness.

"Perhaps the craving beneath our digital addictions isn't content but communion."

Perhaps the craving beneath our digital addictions isn't content but communion. What if our desire for intimacy with God and others is cloaked in the guise of novelty, activity, and performance? What if our hunger isn't for information but to feel something authentic, to be held, seen, known, loved, and met where we hurt and hope?

In the 16th century, Teresa of Ávila imagined the soul as a vast, radiant castle.[19] Within its walls are many rooms, each drawing closer to

---

[19] Teresa of Ávila, *The Interior Castle.*

the One who dwells in the center: the Beloved. To move inward is to journey toward intimacy. To be distracted is to wander the halls endlessly, never reaching the center. The image is old, but the wisdom is timely. If TikTok and other social media are labyrinths of distractions, Teresa offers a map home.

The First Step: Waking Up in the Courtyard

Many live outside the gates of the soul's interior castle, unaware that such a place exists. But some awaken, often through pain, longing, or holy discontent. This is the first mansion: awareness. People realize they're more than their food and that their souls are starving while their minds are saturated. This awakening is grace.

"Awakening to our inadequacy and need isn't a failure of discipline but the beginning of faith, hope, love, and divine grace."

Glimpsing our restlessness is the first step onto holy ground. Awakening to our inadequacy and need isn't a failure of discipline but the beginning of faith, hope, love, and divine grace. When we know at the interior castle's door, we're offering belief, however faintly, that our Creator made us for something eternal and more profound than a distraction.

The first rooms are still noisy. Thoughts buzz. Old patterns cling. But the soul begins to seek silence. Here, the challenge is consistency. Social media trains the brain to crave stimulation every few seconds. Prayer invites a slower rhythm. Teresa would say: don't force deep prayer yet; instead, show up. Come to the castle. Knock. Sit still even if nothing happens. The first rooms are where perseverance is born.

The Battle of the Middle Mansions

As one moves inward, the temptations shift. It's no longer just distraction but discouragement. "Why isn't this working?" "Why do I still feel far from God?" Teresa knew these struggles. She warned of spiritual pride, false consolations, and dryness.[20] But she also wrote of love that grows through fidelity, not fireworks.

In these rooms, the soul learns to let go of performance. Prayer becomes less about achievement and more about presence. The interior castle teaches us that God isn't waiting to be impressed but welcomed. Social media metrics, such as followers, likes, and reach, have no meaning here.[21] What matters is desire, humility, grace, and faithfulness.

"We're learning to love God without fireworks and miracles: to trust in dry prayers, aching hearts, and dim light, knowing God is still near."

As we enter the middle rooms of our interior castle, our faith becomes less about emotions and more about faithfulness: less about spectacle and more about stillness. We're learning to love God without fireworks and miracles and to trust in dry prayers, aching hearts, and dim light, knowing God is still near.

This is where real transformation begins. The noise doesn't stop, but the soul grows less reactive. One learns to pause before clicking, pray before posting, and let silence interrupt the scroll. Little by little, the castle becomes more than a metaphor. It becomes home.

The Center Holds

The innermost room, the seventh mansion, is where union happens: not perfection, not escape, but union with God.[22] This union is a mysterious communion in which the soul and the Beloved are so close that they breathe the same breath. Few speak of this because words can't carry its weight. Teresa tried with trembling joy.

But this union isn't for mystics only. It isn't reserved for cloisters, monks, mystics, or saints. The door is open to anyone who desires God more than distraction: even a soul with a cracked screen and tired eyes. Especially that soul. This is the same Christ who says, "Come to me, all

---

[20] Teresa of Ávila, *The Interior Castle*, Mansions IV–VI.
[21] Newport, *Digital Minimalism*.
[22] Anonymous, *The Cloud of Unknowing*.

who are weary," and invites us not into performance, but into rest, renewal, and resurrection (Matthew 11:28).

The center rooms of our inner heart don't promise ecstasy but a love that comforts, heals, and holds even when the world unravels and the soul feels numb. Living from the center means carrying a stillness that the world can't steal since we're rooted in God's nature, promises, and love, deeper and surer than the feed's churn.

Union doesn't mean every prayer feels electric. Often, it's marked by a trust that endures dryness, confusion, and even God's apparent absence. It's love that stays. In a world where attention flits and loyalties shift, the castle offers rootedness and a place where love holds firm.

Practices for Building Your Interior Castle

How does one build an inner life in the age of TikTok videos, Instagram reels, and YouTube shorts? Not with grand gestures but with daily choices. Spiritual growth involves choosing practices that aren't heroic but humble and that don't just reorient us away from distraction but toward presence, love, and truth. When we practice these habits, we tend to the gardens of our souls. Here are some spiritual habits to help:

1. Sacred Silence

Choose five minutes a day to sit in silence. No music, podcast, phone, internet: just breath and presence. It'll feel awkward at first, but stay anyway. Let the stillness work on you like water shaping stone.

2. Rule of Life

Craft a simple rhythm for your days: morning prayer, digital curfews, a tech-free hour, and walks without earbuds. The soul thrives on rhythm, while social media thrives on disruption. Choose your master.

3. Lectio Divina

Let Scripture become a mirror. Read slowly. Pause. Listen. Ask, "What's God saying to me today?" Don't rush for answers. Let the Word read you.

4. Digital Discernment

Before you open an app, ask: What am I looking for? Connection? Comfort? Escape? Distraction? Applause? Assurance? Bring that longing to prayer. You might find the craving behind the scroll is a cry for God.

5. Companions for the Journey

You can't walk the castle alone. Find spiritual friends. A mentor. A community. People who long for depth ask hard questions and hold sacred silence with you. You don't need many, just a few companions who keep you faithful.

A Holy Resistance

To build an interior castle is to resist the tyranny of noise.[23] It's a quiet rebellion against the algorithms that profit from your addiction. It's saying, "My soul isn't for sale. My mind isn't your playground. I was made for union, not consumption."

"You don't have to flee the digital world. But you do have to choose how you inhabit it."

You don't have to flee the digital world. But you do have to choose how you inhabit it. Bring your soul online. Bring your presence. Be contemplative on the timeline. Be the one who listens more than reacts, posts from prayer, and pauses before clicking.

Resistance isn't anger; it's reverence. Subversion isn't unholy; it's surrender. Reclaiming your attention proclaims your soul is sacred, not programmable or monetizable. As we live contemplatively online, we disrupt the algorithms with grace. We choose to post from prayer, engage

---

23 Jacobs, *Breaking Bread with the Dead.*

from peace, and bless from love. From this interior grounding, we're also sent out to love more boldly, serve more freely, and speak truth with grace in a noisy world. In every pause before the scroll, in every breath taken before a click, we proclaim that we belong not to platforms but to Love.

Teresa wouldn't ask you to leave your generation behind. She would invite you deeper: past the flashing images and the curated self, into the truth of who you are and the mystery of God, who waits for you not in pixels but in presence.

The Castle Is Already Within

You don't have to build the castle from scratch. It's already there, planted in you like a seed, hidden beneath layers of noise, fear, and forgetfulness. But it waits.

Christ, our Beloved, waits: not far off, but within. Closer than your next notification, deeper than your latest distraction. The One who died and rose to make your soul his home is calling you inward: not to escape, but to be transformed.

So, silence the screen. Light a candle. Offer a prayer. And begin again. One room at a time. Toward the center. Toward the One who has always been waiting for intimacy with you.

You aren't your screen time. You aren't your follower count. You're a soul. A castle. A home for the holy, loving God.

"You aren't your screen time. You aren't your follower count. You're a soul. A castle. A home for the holy, loving God."

And you're already being drawn inward into love.

PART II — SPIRIT, WORD, AND TRUTH: DISCERNMENT AND DEPTH

Part 2 plays with paradox (reason and mystery, speech and silence, truth and humility) in the midst of cultural division and noise.

6. Critical Theory and the Cloud of Unknowing

We live in a time when tables meant for communion have become battlegrounds. Conversations that should nourish have turned into debates that devour. Topics like race, equity, gender, and justice, which were once the heart of prophetic witness and pastoral care, now spark fear, anger, and division. Words that once inspired have been weaponized. Language is currency and combat. And many have stopped speaking altogether, not because they don't care, but because they're weary, cautious, or afraid of being misunderstood.

But what if the invitation isn't to argue better but to listen deeper? What if what we need right now isn't more data or debate but a descent into the cloud?

Weaponized words create weary, fearful, angry, silenced souls. Our hearts need something deeper than conflicted or ideological discourse. Speaking the truth in love isn't the same as performing certainty; the former invites relationship and transformation, and the latter demands posturing and applause. Jesus showed us that tables aren't places to win arguments but to wash feet.

The 14th-century anonymous mystic who wrote *The Cloud of Unknowing* offered an apophatic path: a way of knowing that begins in unknowing, of moving closer to God not through mastery but through surrender.[24] What if that wisdom could guide our theology and engagement with justice, identity, and difference?

---

[24] Anonymous. *The Cloud of Unknowing.*

The Humble Descent of Unknowing

To speak of *the cloud of unknowing* is to imagine a spiritual path where the soul no longer seeks to grasp God through thought but to rest in God through love. It's the sacred unlearning of all we think we know, the gentle surrender of images, words, and certainties until we're left with nothing but a profound longing. This longing becomes prayer. In this cloud, God isn't absent but hidden, not unknowable but beyond knowing. The heart, stripped of all but desire, beats gently against the mystery, trusting that love alone can carry it across the threshold. Here, in the soft darkness of holy unknowing, we don't find answers; we find God's presence and love. And in that sacred presence, God sees us and calls us beloved.

"You can't think your way to God. You can only love your way to God."

Here's the key idea: *You can't think your way to God. You can only love your way to God.*[25]

The mystics speak of a humility that isn't weakness but wonder.[26] In the apophatic tradition, you don't approach the Holy with clenched fists or sharpened arguments. You come open-handed, acknowledging that you don't know. You can't control. You can't conquer mystery. You can only be drawn.

To enter the holy cloud of unknowing isn't to abandon truth or divine revelation but to bow before the holiness and wonder of mystery that refuses to be domesticated, defined, and mastered. The descent isn't a fall from clarity but a pilgrimage into presence, which frees us from needing to reason, define, master, and know and, instead, opens us to

---

[25] One of the foundational principles from *The Cloud of Unknowing* is that only a "dart of longing love" can pierce the cloud between the soul and God. The central teaching of *The Cloud of Unknowing* is that God is known not through intellect but through the movement of love beyond knowing.

[26] Starr, trans. *The Interior Castle.*

love. The cloud isn't the absence of God but the refusal of idolatry: letting go of thoughts and images that shrink God into our control.

The descent into unknowing isn't the abandonment of Scripture, but the deepening of its mystery: where truth isn't flattened into slogans but lived in love.

"This is the posture we need in polarized times; not a disengaged relativism but a holy unknowing; not giving up but giving over."

This is the posture we need in polarized times; not a disengaged relativism but a holy unknowing; not giving up but giving over. It's the kind of humility that dares to enter complexity without demanding clarity too soon and holds space for grief, rage, joy, and ambiguity without rushing to resolution.

If we approached conversations about race, privilege, history, and harm with that kind of soul, how different might they sound? How might we speak if we saw the person across the table not as a threat or project but as a mystery animated by divine breath? How might we listen?

The False Security of Certainty

The temptation is to retreat into echo chambers where our perspectives are mirrored and confirmed or to rush into the fray with all the right terms and trending theories, convinced that if we can name the system, we've solved the problem.

But systems aren't solved by ideology alone. They're transformed by hearts softened by grace. Certainty can become a kind of idolatry: an armor we wear to avoid vulnerability. Certainty has its place, but it must be held with humility and shaped by love, not fear. Transformation never comes to the armored. It comes to those willing to be wounded by love. Our systems of thought don't save us; only God's grace can.

"Certainty can become a kind of idolatry: an armor we wear to avoid vulnerability. Certainty has its place, but it must be held with humility and shaped by love, not fear."

The cloud reminds us that God is best approached not by the intellect alone but by a "dart of longing love."[27] Love that's ungrasping and unclenching must shape our justice work. Critical theory has tools, but the mystic carries presence. Some frameworks help us name injustice and systems of harm, but without love, even the sharpest analysis can miss the heart. A presence that's kind, open, inclusive, quiet, grounded, and attentive is what most hearts long for in the middle of this noise.

Sacred Listening as Resistance

In the contemplative path, silence isn't absence. It's attention.[28] It's resistance against the culture of reaction. It's the choice to wait in love before speaking.

This kind of listening doesn't tune out. It tunes in. It's the listening that hears the cry beneath the critique, the wound beneath the rage, and the yearning beneath the cynicism. This kind of listening becomes a sacrament: a way of being present to Christ hidden in the other, especially the one who challenges or confronts us.[29]

Silence can make us attentive and soften our hearts. It can help us be soft enough to see and carry others' pain without turning to accusations or defense. In sacred listening, we don't lose conviction; we locate it in grace and love.

Contemplation doesn't replace activism; it roots it. The quiet strength of prayer becomes the courage to stand with the oppressed, not just speak about them.

Imagine what it would be like if the church became known not just for statements and stances but for sacred listening. Imagine what it'd be like if we were known for communities where people don't have to edit their pain, sanitize their stories, or silence their questions. Imagine a

---

27 This phrase is drawn directly from *The Cloud of Unknowing*, describing the soul's movement toward God as not rational but driven by love.
28 Main, *Word into Silence*.
29 Influenced by John Main's work in contemplative silence, especially his notion of listening as participation in the divine Word. Main, *Word into Silence*.

church where truth and love walk hand in hand and where justice is born from compassion, not conquest.

The Cloud Between Us

The Cloud of Unknowing tells us to let go of every image, concept, and assumption and to pierce the cloud not with thought but with love. That same discipline is needed in our human relationships, especially in fraught conversations.

To enter the cloud between us means letting go of our pre-formed conclusions about the other. It means releasing the need to be right, liked, or in control. It means being willing to dwell in the discomfort of not knowing long enough to let something holy emerge.

"Some conversations require more than courage. They require contemplation."

Some conversations require more than courage. They require contemplation. A heart trained in the silence of God's presence can hear more than words. It can feel the weight of another's story. It can hold complexity without collapsing into chaos.

This doesn't mean abandoning conviction. It means anchoring conviction in love and grace. It means recognizing that true clarity often only comes after the cloud, not before it. It means refusing to weaponize the Bible, theology, or justice as ways to dominate but reclaiming them as ways to serve.

The Slow Work of Union

The mystics never rushed. They knew that love takes time and communion is formed slowly, like bread rising in the dark.[30]

Justice is slow work, too.[31] So is reconciliation. So is healing. And in that slowness, we need spaces where the Spirit can whisper and

---

[30] Teresa of Ávila, *The Interior Castle*.
[31] This resonates with the mystic tradition's emphasis on slow, transformative communion, and with practices of justice grounded in presence rather than urgency.

breathe. Where confession is welcomed, not weaponized. Where forgiveness flows but is never forced. Where truth isn't rushed, and grace isn't cheap.

"Justice is slow work, too. So is reconciliation. So is healing."

The mystics remind us that the deepest change comes not through coercion but through union: not just knowing about the other but becoming bound to them in the heart of Christ. That kind of unity requires more than shared opinions. It requires shared surrender.

Love in the Fog

We're living through a thick fog of misinformation, trauma, history, and broken trust. But even here, love moves. Even here, the Spirit hovers.

Even when we can't see the road, we're still invited to walk it by faith, not sight, and by love, not fear. The fog doesn't hinder love; it deepens its reach, forcing us to trust what can't be proven but is deeply known. Our healing won't be found in a perfect argument but in a faithful presence that refuses to let go.

So, let's enter the cloud, not to escape the world but to love it more truly. Let's unlearn some things so we can receive new wisdom. Let's listen not to win but to be changed. Let's practice justice that isn't reactive but radiant: justice shaped by prayer, presence, and love's patient, slow courage.

Because, in the end, the cloud doesn't last forever. It leads to light. Not the harsh light of scrutiny but the soft light of communion. The light that shows us not just what's wrong but who we are: beloved, wounded, and called to walk with each other toward healing.

There's hope in the cloud. Not because we see clearly but because we trust the One who does. And in that trust, we walk: not with certainty, but with love.

7. The Sacred Gift of Free Speech: Why it Must Be Guarded with Truth and Grace

Words create worlds. From the first breath of creation, when divine speech summoned light from the void, to the prayers of the weary and the fiery declarations of the prophets, human history has been shaped by speech.[32] Words carry spirit. They form, reveal, and bind; they can also fracture, deceive, and destroy. In a culture overwhelmed by noise, outrage, and misinformation, the sacredness of speech is easily overlooked. We speak to win, to wound, to dominate, and call it freedom. Yet the Christian tradition teaches that freedom of speech isn't a license for cruelty or a weapon for power. It's a vocation rooted in love, truth, and the dignity of every person created in the image of God.

Free speech matters not only because it preserves democracy, but because it protects the soul of a people. To silence conscience, suppress truth, or censor dissent is to erase part of the divine image within us: the part that seeks, questions, and speaks. Yet freedom itself is fragile. It must be guarded not only against authoritarian control but also against moral corrosion from within: when our words no longer serve truth or love, when freedom is twisted into permission to harm.

We live in a moment when speech has become weaponized, when words that should build bridges are turned into bludgeons. Political tribes speak in echo chambers. Outrage has become currency. And yet, beneath

---

[32] Genesis 1:3.

the shouting, there remains a yearning: a longing for voices that heal, not hurt; for truth that liberates, not manipulates.

"Free speech is sacred not because it allows us to say anything, but because it calls us to say what is true, healing, and just."

Words That Create, Words That Destroy

In Scripture, speech is never neutral. "Let there be light," God said, and there was light. Creation itself is the result of a divine sentence. Likewise, when we speak, we participate in the mystery of creation: our words shape the moral and emotional climate of the world around us. The letter of James compares the tongue to a spark that can set a forest ablaze, and to a rudder that can steer the course of a great ship.[33] Speech builds empires and breaks them; it reconciles nations and provokes wars.

When societies lose the ability to speak truthfully, they lose their moral compass. Lies breed fear, fear breeds violence, and violence breeds silence. The health of a democracy depends not only on its institutions and laws, but also on the honesty of its citizens: their willingness to speak the truth and to listen with humility.

However, we now live in an era of linguistic inflation: words are cheap, abundant, and easily weaponized. Misinformation travels faster than facts; insults outpace insight. We no longer pause to discern truth before we speak. And when words lose meaning, freedom itself begins to decay.

The Spiritual Weight of Speech

The Christian vision reminds us that words are spiritual acts. They either reveal the image of God or distort it. "Out of the abundance of the heart the mouth speaks," said Jesus.[34] Every careless word exposes something of our interior world. Speech, then, isn't merely a civil liberty; it's a spiritual discipline.

---

[33] James 3:5–6.
[34] Matthew 12:34.

"When speech is detached from truth, it becomes violence; when it's detached from love, it becomes manipulation."

When speech becomes detached from truth, it becomes violence. When it's detached from love, it becomes manipulation. But when truth and love are joined, speech becomes sacrament: it mediates grace, reconciles enemies, and participates in divine healing.

This is why free speech is sacred. It acknowledges that each person, regardless of belief or background, bears within them the capacity to speak truth. It protects the conscience, allowing individuals to name what is right and resist what is wrong. In this sense, freedom of speech is a spiritual safeguard: it defends the space where truth can contend with falsehood and light can challenge darkness.

Yet speech, like all sacred gifts, can be desecrated. We desecrate it when we use it to degrade others, when we mock, lie, or vilify. We desecrate it when we use "freedom" as a cloak for cruelty.

The Peril of Weaponized Freedom

The paradox of our age is that speech is freer than ever and yet more distorted. Many now mistake volume for truth, cruelty for courage, and outrage for integrity. Freedom of expression has become a slogan detached from moral responsibility.

"True freedom of speech doesn't thrive in chaos; it flourishes where humility and courage meet."

But true freedom of speech doesn't mean the absence of restraint; it implies the presence of virtue. Freedom divorced from truth becomes tyranny of another kind. The prophets warned of those who "call evil good and good evil," who "make lies their refuge."[35] They knew that speech can corrupt a nation when it ceases to be accountable to God and neighbor.

---

[35] Isaiah 5:20; 28:15.

When people use speech to humiliate or incite hatred, freedom becomes domination. When leaders exploit free speech to spread lies or sow fear, they betray the very liberty they claim to defend. The danger isn't only political but spiritual: when the public square becomes a battlefield of vengeance, our souls grow calloused, and the truth itself becomes a casualty.

The task, then, isn't to limit speech but to elevate it: to cultivate a moral imagination where freedom is exercised in service of love.

Jesus and the Freedom to Speak Truth

Jesus of Nazareth stood before emperors and priests with nothing but words and changed the world. His speech was both tender and unsettling, filled with mercy and judgment. He spoke in parables that revealed the heart and exposed hypocrisy. He confronted oppressive systems not with swords or slogans but with the sharpness of truth.

Yet Jesus also understood the discipline of silence. When accused before Pilate, he didn't argue or retaliate. His silence wasn't weakness; it was a rebuke to the powers that confuse noise with authority. In that silence, truth stood taller than the empire.

"Jesus spoke truth to power, but he also knew when silence could say more than speech."

The life of Jesus reveals that speech and silence both have holy purposes. There's a time to speak truth to power, and a time to remain still before mystery. Both resist the tyranny of vengeance and the idolatry of control.

On the cross, Jesus gave the most subversive word ever spoken: "Father, forgive them, for they know not what they do."[36] In that prayer, the language of vengeance was replaced with the language of mercy. Free speech finds its truest form here: not in the freedom to retaliate, but in the freedom to speak the truth in love and to forgive.

---

[36] Luke 23:34.

Why Free Speech Must Be Guarded for All

Free speech must be defended not only for those we agree with but also for those we can't stand to hear. Once the right to speak is limited to the favored or the powerful, the prophetic voice is endangered. History teaches this with painful clarity: whenever regimes or movements (religious or secular) have silenced dissent in the name of order or purity, violence soon follows.

The prophets were often unpopular because they told uncomfortable truths. Jeremiah was jailed, Amos was exiled, and Jesus was crucified. A society that suppresses speech in the name of safety or ideology eventually silences conscience itself.

But defending free speech doesn't mean tolerating lies or hate without response. It means meeting bad speech with better speech, falsehood with truth, hatred with reasoned love. The solution to poisonous words isn't censorship but conversion: a moral renewal that changes how we speak and hear one another.

This is why freedom of speech must be preserved for all people, not as a political slogan but as a moral covenant. It's the shared trust that allows communities to deliberate, repent, forgive, and grow. Without it, truth withers in secrecy, and power goes unchecked.

Words are holy things. They can build or burn, bless or blaspheme. If free speech is sacred because words create worlds, then we must also ask what kind of world our words are creating. Every freedom carries responsibility, and every tongue has power. To cherish free speech means not only defending it but discerning it: learning when speech brings life, and when it tears the fabric of truth apart.

Freedom and Its Boundaries: Speaking Truth Without Harm

Freedom of speech is precious, but it's not absolute. Every freedom carries a moral horizon: a boundary shaped not by fear or censorship, but by love. Christian faith insists that liberty finds its truest expression not in doing whatever we please, but in serving the good of others.

"Everything is permissible," Paul once wrote, "but not everything is beneficial."[37] Freedom unmoored from love becomes chaos; love without freedom becomes a form of control. The tension between the two is where moral maturity lives.

In a democracy, free speech must remain broad enough to accommodate disagreement, dissent, and even offense. The prophets were often offensive to kings. Jesus unsettled the powerful with his words. Truth will always sting before it heals. But the purpose of speech (in public life and in faith) isn't to humiliate, inflame, or destroy. It's to build a common life where truth and mercy meet, where disagreement becomes the forge of wisdom, not the spark of violence.

The Christian vision calls us to discern the difference between speech that wounds to heal and speech that wounds to harm. A prophet's rebuke tears down idols so that justice can rise. But words that demean, dehumanize, or incite hatred don't liberate; they enslave. They serve the same spirit that nailed the Truth to a cross. Every time speech becomes a weapon against the vulnerable, it betrays both democracy and discipleship.

To follow Jesus is to speak truth, but always cruciform truth: truth carried in humility, restraint, and love. Christ knew when to challenge ("You brood of vipers") and when to be silent ("He answered him not a word"). His silence before Pilate wasn't a sign of weakness; it was a form of resistance. It revealed that not every provocation warrants a response, and that sometimes the most effective speech is self-control. In that stillness, he bore witness to a freedom deeper than expression: the freedom of a heart anchored in God's peace.

In our time, defending free speech must include defending the conditions that allow truth to flourish: honesty, humility, and compassion. We must protect the right to speak, even for those with whom we disagree. However, we must also reject the notion that cruelty is a form of courage or that hatred is a form of honesty. Free speech isn't

---

[37] 1 Corinthians 10:23.

a license for contempt. It's a sacred trust that binds our tongues to the service of truth and the dignity of every human being.

To guard that trust is the work of both conscience and community. It requires courage to speak, wisdom to listen, and humility to learn. It demands that people of faith model a better use of words: words that challenge without condemning, correct without shaming, reveal truth without erasing grace. When speech serves love, it becomes a sacrament: a small sign of God's Word still speaking to the world toward healing.

The Practice of Holy Speech

If free speech is sacred, it demands spiritual discipline. How, then, do we speak in ways that honor both freedom and love?

1. Speak with Reverence

Before speaking, remember that words can either echo the Word or echo chaos. Treat speech as prayer: pause, discern, and ask if your words will build up or break down.

2. Listen Before You Speak

Silence is the first act of respect. Listening doesn't mean agreement; it means acknowledging the divine image in another. Listening is how love learns to speak.

3. Tell the Truth, Even When It Costs You

Free speech without courage is hollow. In a culture addicted to flattery and fear, truth-telling is an act of faith. Speak with integrity, even when it isolates you. The truth may wound, but lies destroy.

4. Refuse the Language of Contempt

Contempt corrodes dialogue. Never mock, demean, or reduce others to caricatures. Jesus rebuked his disciples when they wanted to call fire down from heaven on their enemies. He calls us instead to a different fire: the fire of the Spirit that purifies, not destroys.

5. Use Speech for Healing

Let your words be medicine. In a divided world, speak words that reconcile, comfort, and humanize. Speak against injustice, but do so in a spirit that longs for redemption, not revenge.

6. Practice the Art of Silence

In moments of anger, silence can be the truest form of resistance. To refrain from hateful speech isn't cowardice but courage. Silence can create a sacred space where the Spirit offers wisdom.

The Fragility and Beauty of Democratic Speech

Democracy depends on the same virtues that faith requires: humility, patience, and courage. Free speech isn't only the right to speak your mind; it's the discipline of listening to voices that unsettle you. Without that discipline, societies polarize into tribes that can no longer reason together.

The task of sustaining free speech is as spiritual as it's political. It requires citizens formed by habits of honesty and empathy. It requires institutions that protect dissent, and a people who resist the seduction of propaganda.

When we lose the ability to speak freely and truthfully, democracy degenerates into a performance, where leaders exploit outrage, and citizens become spectators instead of participants. But when we reclaim speech as a moral act, public life can once again become a space of shared meaning and hope.

A Mystical Vision of Word and Silence

Christian mysticism has long recognized that words and silence are inextricably linked.[38] The Word became flesh not to drown the world in noise but to reveal love through presence. God's speech in Christ wasn't domination but incarnation: truth clothed in tenderness.

---

[38] Teresa of Ávila, *The Interior Castle*; Anonymous, *The Cloud of Unknowing*.

When we speak with this awareness, speech becomes a form of communion. It's no longer about winning or persuading but about encountering the other as sacred. In that encounter, free speech fulfills its deepest purpose: not self-expression, but self-giving.

Imagine a public square where speech is shaped by this contemplative vision: where voices rise not to dominate but to dialogue; where the truth is spoken with mercy; where silence isn't fear but reverence. That's the kind of world the gospel imagines: not a world without conflict, but one where conflict is humanized by compassion.

The Cross and the Renewal of Speech

The cross is the ultimate test of speech. It shows what happens when truth is silenced and lies prevail. Yet it also shows the victory of love's word over hate's noise. At Calvary, the world's violence tried to cancel the Word of God, but the resurrection proved that truth can't be silenced forever.

This is why followers of Jesus (and all who seek peace) must become guardians of the Word. We must speak life into the voids of our culture, name injustice without hatred, and defend the dignity of even those whose speech offends us.

The alternative to free speech is tyranny and chaos. The challenge, then, is to live in the tension: to speak boldly yet humbly, to love fiercely yet wisely, to use our freedom for healing and not harm.

Free Speech is a Moral and Spiritual Calling

Free speech isn't merely a democratic or constitutional right; it's a moral and spiritual calling. It's the freedom to bear witness to truth, to love, to grace, and to the human of all others. It's the space where repentance, respect, and renewal become possible.

"Every time we speak truthfully, humbly, and with love, the Word becomes flesh again in our midst."

The words we speak will either heal or wound, build or destroy, reconcile or divide. Our task is to choose which language we will speak: the language of vengeance or the language of grace; the language of fear or the language of hope.

The Word became flesh and dwelt among us, speaking peace into violence and mercy into hatred. Every time we speak truthfully, humbly, and with love, that same Word takes flesh again in our midst. Every time we champion free speech, we honor the image of God in every human being.

So let's guard this sacred freedom with reverence. Let's speak as those who know that words create worlds and that, in the end, the truest speech is love made audible.

8. Four Ways to Live in the Power of the Spirit and Word

Jesus replied, "You are in error because you don't know the Scriptures or the power of God." (Matthew 22:29).

Spirit baptism has been a defining experience in my discipleship to Jesus Christ. I remember the night well. I was sixteen, angry, wounded, and insecure. I had just attended a Pentecostal worship service and had responded to the pastor's invitation to receive Spirit baptism. Nothing happened to me when the pastor prayed.

That night, alone in my room, I cried out to God for his presence. Around midnight, I experienced the Spirit's power and presence intensely and overwhelmingly. It wasn't "speaking in tongues" that impressed me: I felt overwhelmed by the direct experience of God's love, grace, forgiveness, healing, assurance, hope, joy, and empowering presence. Since then, I have had a strong desire to experience the transforming and empowering presence of the Spirit.

Many years ago, a friend introduced me to the work of R.T. Kendall, a pastor and writer who served as pastor of Westminster Chapel for twenty-five years. He is the author of over fifty books and an engaging writer and communicator.

I don't agree with everything R.T. Kendall writes, and I don't always agree with his interpretation of Scripture. However, his primary thesis has struck me forcefully: there has been a "silent divorce" in the church between the Word and the Spirit, and these must be brought back together for the church to be healthy and biblical. Today, the church must recover the power of the combined and inseparable Word and Spirit.

I can see the separation R.T. Kendall is talking about in my own life and experience of the church. I came to faith in Pentecostalism and spent years experiencing the power and presence of the Holy Spirit in prophecy, spiritual passion, healing, boldness for witness, and expectant faith. However, the attention to sound biblical knowledge and interpretation was often weak. I then transitioned to Evangelical churches and spent years experiencing solid teaching, expository preaching, a sound understanding, and a high view of Scripture. But the attention to the Holy Spirit's power, presence, leading, and renewal was often non-existent or weak. In other words, I experienced first-hand the effects of the separation of Word and Spirit in the church.

Lately, I've asked myself, "How can we bring the Word and the Spirit back together so Christians can experience the life-changing, world-transforming effects of God's truth and power?"

Here are four ways we can do this.

Seek to *Know* Both the Scriptures and the Power of God

In Matthew 22:23–33, Jesus engages the Sadducees in a debate about marriage at the resurrection. He strikes these religious leaders with these words: "You are in error because you don't know the Scriptures or the power of God." Jesus thinks that these religious leaders don't even know what the Scriptures say about the resurrection, let alone the power of God to do supernatural, astonishing, world-transforming things.

Their errors of biblical interpretation and superficial, corrupted faith arise directly from the fact that they don't know the Scriptures or the power of God. Yet, Jesus knew both. In verse 33, we see that the crowds were "astonished" (amazed) when they heard him (as in Luke 9:43 and Acts 3:10). Jesus could amaze with his words as quickly as with his signs and wonders – both produced the same reaction. This is because Jesus walked in the power of the Word and the Spirit. We must seek to know both, too.

Seek to *Integrate* the Word and the Spirit, in Faith and Life

The Spirit doesn't only mean miracles, signs, and wonders, and the Word doesn't only imply exposition and doctrine. That would draw the distinction too sharply: the two are always integrated.

Christians discover life and God's empowering presence when they integrate the Word and Spirit in every part of their community, witness, and life. God is honored and glorified when two things coalesce: the Scriptures and the power of God. These can't be kept apart or in isolation from one another. Bringing the two together sets a fire in the hearts of believers and the church: it ignites the mission, hope, faith, love, community, joy, and witness of God's people.

Some theologians argue that it's impossible to separate the Word and the Spirit. In one sense, this is true. But in another sense, it's possible to deliver the Word without the power of the Spirit, and vice versa.

Jesus said that the Sadducees were ignorant of both Word and power: but with some in the present day, it's either ignorance of one or the other. Some detect heresy or cold orthodoxy a mile away but can't see what is missing in their tradition. Neither of these emphases on Spirit or Word is wrong, but they must be married together!

Our churches and ministries will continue to struggle while we neglect either the Word or the Spirit. The church will continue to struggle until it's not one or the other but passionate and committed to Scripture and the Holy Spirit's power.

Seek to *Relinquish* Spiritual Pride and an Unteachable Spirit

Getting Pentecostals (or charismatic and renewalist movements) to learn from Evangelicals (Word-centered movements) and vice versa can be challenging. Both sides often think they're right and have nothing to learn from the other. But we need to relinquish this spiritual pride, isolationism, and unteachable spirit.

The Sadducees said that there is no resurrection of the body. They had little respect for the prophetic or the power of God. They embraced a dead, legalistic orthodoxy. They were determined to claim that their doctrinal distinctives were correct and that Jesus of Nazareth was to be ignored.

But Jesus says that this kind of religiosity is a deception. This religiosity and spiritual pride are expressed in both Spirit and Word movements. Jesus said that they were in error because they were "deceived": they arrogantly thought they were right, but they did not know the Scriptures or the power of God.

God wants nothing to do with spiritual pride: neither in one's spiritual power nor in one's biblical orthodoxy.

The Sadducees' unteachable spirit and religious pride led to ignorance: they weren't even acquainted with what they claimed to be experts on. Here's something that worries me greatly. We have a generation of people who don't know their Bibles and a generation who are equally ignorant of God's power. We must address this issue, and it begins with relinquishing academic, Evangelical, or Pentecostal pride (all forms of spiritual pride!) and embracing teachable hearts and humility.

Seek to *Live* Daily in the Life-Changing, World-Transforming Power of the Spirit and the Word

As a former pastor and teacher at a theological college, I need to constantly ask myself: "Am I seeking to experience and live in God's power and presence? Does God's empowering presence infuse, enliven, and animate my teaching? And is this desire for God's power and presence truly integrated with a passion for God's Word?"

We all need to ask ourselves these kinds of questions regularly.

Living in the power of the Word and Spirit isn't just about biblical study and confidence in Scripture or about signs and wonders and the gifts of the Spirit. Living in the life of the Word and Spirit is about fighting injustice, confronting exploitation, caring for creation, welcoming the stranger, and seeing the Spirit in art, beauty, culture, and the world around us. It's about confronting race, prejudice, discrimination, and reconciliation.

Over thirty years of ministry, I've learned that sound doctrine, expository preaching, and a high view of Scripture are critical. But we must also recover spiritual vitality and power, the power and gifts of the Holy Spirit. These two must not only coincide; they must be integrated and inseparable from each other.

Living in the power of the Word and Spirit is about expressing the fruit of the Spirit, being generous and content, caring for the poor and broken, and loving our enemies. Living in the power of the Word and Spirit is about embracing the radical social ethics of the Sermon on the Mount and the Beatitudes. It's about being a people who live lives (together and in the world) that alert people to God's universal rule and reign. It's about letting go of old dichotomies (Word–Spirit, sacred-secular, proclamation–social justice, and so on) and embracing the integral and integrative life of the Spirit. It's about living in a posture of discernment and attention: keeping in step with the Spirit and walking in daily dependence on his leadership, presence, and power.

What happens when Christians embrace both the Word and Spirit? God is glorified, lives are transformed, mission is accomplished, community is revitalized, and the church experiences God's empowering presence (God's holy, purifying, true, emboldening, and transforming presence).

9. Twelve Ways to Follow Jesus and Reimagine Evangelicalism in a Secular Age

I'm an evangelical Christian, with roots in biblical theology, Christian spiritual traditions, Pentecostal practices, and progressive politics.

I love the things that evangelicals hold dear: the joyous transformation of personal conversion, the centrality and supremacy of Christ, the power of the gospel, the authority of the Bible, and the call to evangelism and making a difference in society.

At its best, evangelicalism offers an extraordinary and compelling vision for life and faith. There are more than six hundred million evangelicals worldwide; more if you add Pentecostal and charismatic movements that hold the same convictions as those who call themselves evangelical.

But "evangelical" has become a dirty word in many circles. It's become associated with a wide range of negative ideas and themes, especially, but not only, in the United States. There are many examples. Promoting partisan politics. Fearing cultural change. Rejecting those who do hold to a rigid form of Calvinism. Embracing nationalism and sanctioning militarism. Encouraging racial and gender discrimination. Acting as moral police while avoiding real scrutiny. Equating white middle-class values and lifestyles with the gospel. Avoiding scholarship and independent thought. Conflating capitalism with the Christian good life. Being afraid of science and literature and higher criticism. Endorsing immoral politicians and forming questionable alliances for short-term social or political gain. The list is long.

In many circles, evangelicals are seen as jerks, or worse.

So, if you ask me what I mean when I say "I'm an evangelical", I'll need to offer some explanation.

If by evangelical you mean a certain kind of narrow, fear-based, exclusive, partisan, politicized, and combative faith, then, no, I'm not that kind of evangelical. But if by evangelical you mean a generous, inclusive, humble, and love-based commitment to people and the gospel, then, yes, that's my kind of evangelicalism.

The Bible is the highest authority in Christian life; people need the salvation offered only through the gospel and person of Jesus Christ; and God calls us to proclaim Christ and his salvation in every way possible. But none of that needs to be associated with the problems I've just mentioned.

Some friends ask me, "Are you an evangelical?" Yes, I am, and a conservative one. But I have no time for some forms of evangelicalism that are combative, politicized, small-minded, and ungracious. I think being a conservative evangelical involves a commitment to Christ, evangelism, gospel-faithfulness and Scripture; and also to social justice, cultural renewal, racial and gender justice, ministering in the power of the Spirit, holistic ministry, political action, creation care, peacemaking, and reconciliation. This is a generous and embracing evangelicalism that is truer to the gospel and to the witness of Jesus.

In Inigo Montoya's words, sometimes I feel like saying, "Evangelical. You keep using that word. I don't think it means what you think it means."

So, what does a generous, loving, humble, and holistic evangelicalism look like? Or, to put it more crassly, how can evangelicals avoid being fearful, moralistic, politicized jerks?

Here are twelve ways to be truly evangelical. These twelve practices aren't the private property of any tribe; they're ordinary Christian faithfulness for the whole church. They rise from Scripture's wide river (from creation to new creation) and speak to every disciple who longs to love Jesus with heart, mind, soul, and strength. Whether you call yourself evangelical, Pentecostal, Catholic, Orthodox, mainline, or simply Christian, the summons is the same: receive the whole gospel, let Scripture lead you deeper into Christ, tear down false divides, listen across cultures, unite Spirit, Word, and justice, embody peace, pursue restored justice, and tend creation as a sacred trust. These aren't partisan talking points; they're the shape of cruciform love in public. In a fractured age, they name a way of life open to all who want their allegiance to belong first and last to the living Christ.

Grasp and Respond to a Fuller Gospel

Evangelicals as passionate about the gospel. But, too often, the gospel is defined in a narrow or prescriptive way. We offer people a small five-point gospel, or something similar. But that's an inadequate or truncated version of the gospel.

Evangelicals must care about the whole biblical witness and the whole gospel. There is no gospel without the full biblical story.

God calls us to repentance and discipleship in response to a grand story. This is the story of creation, of biblical Israel, and of the Jewish Jesus. It's the story of God, from creation to the final rule and reign of Jesus Christ.

So, what is the gospel? The gospel is the climax of this grand, stunning, defining story-a story that spans history, from creation to the eschaton.

1 Corinthians 15:3–4 tells us that the gospel is "of first importance." What is the gospel? "Christ died for our sins in accordance with the Scriptures, he was buried, and he was raised on the third day in accordance with the Scriptures." How does this gospel shape our lives? "For Christ's love compels us, because we're convinced that one died for all, and therefore all died. And he died for all, that those who live should no longer live for themselves but for him who died for them and was raised again."

God calls us to respond to the entire biblical story (creation to eschaton). In one sense, this whole narrative is both the story of Jesus and the gospel. But, in another sense, the gospel is the climax of that story, as revealed in the person and work of Jesus Christ.

The entire, defining, biblical story describes our being. It frames our identity. It determines our purpose. It gives us our mission. And it reveals our hope. This story shapes our vision of community and mission. This grand biblical story must frame, infuse, and shape everything we say and do.

This so much more than a truncated five-point gospel.

The gospel story extends from creation to the end of history and the consummation of God's kingdom. We must be gripped by a vision of the whole biblical witness and story. At the same time, we must honor the climax of that story, in the person and work of Jesus Christ. So, the gospel calls us to attend to personal salvation and the restoration of all things in Christ. The gospel is an invitation to join the story of the triune God, of biblical Israel, of the Jewish Jesus, and of God's reign. A great story shapes our vision for discipleship, mission, ethics, and community. And the gospel is the climax of that story.

A fuller grasp of the gospel leads us to care not only for personal salvation, but also for justice, creation, peace-making, reconciliation, and more. The whole biblical witness and story calls us to care for these things.

Let the Bible Lead to a Deeper Love for Jesus

The Bible is crucial for Christian life. The Bible plumbs, measures, illuminates, adjudicates, enlivens, inspires, norms, and more. The Scriptures are the authoritative word of God, inspired by the Holy Spirit. They have absolute and final authority in all aspects of corporate and individual faith, ethics, conduct, witness, and theology.

Evangelicals must not shy away from biblical authority-we embrace it. Sadly, many western Christians have a declining passion for memorizing and contemplating and interpreting and applying Scripture.

I find this deeply concerning. When I serve in Asia and Africa and Latin America, I see the opposite. People are passionate for Scripture. They devour and honor and memorize it. They interpret it contextually, while maintaining a conservative bias. And they apply it creatively and bravely. This is instructive for those of us in the West. We need a revival in our enthusiasm for Scripture.

But this isn't about "falling in love" with Scripture. It's about devouring Scripture as a means of knowing and adoring and following and loving and magnifying our Lord Jesus Christ.

Tear Down False Divides and Really Join God's Mission

The missional God has a missional church. The church doesn't have its own mission. God has a mission, and the church joins that mission.

But is that mission only about personal and individual conversion? Not at all. Since the mission of God includes the restoration of all things in fellowship with God, our mission must be integral and holistic. It can't just be about simple proclamation or individual conversion. It includes those things but isn't limited to them.

We join the messianic mission of the Son, in the power of the Spirit, to the glory of the Father. Such mission dismantles all polarities and oppositional binaries. We reject proclamation without social justice, or vice versa. We tear down false divides, such as evangelism-justice, sacred-secular, proclamation-action, practical-theological, Word-Spirit, and more.

True evangelical life and mission integrates proclamation, justice, healing, creation care, political action, signs and wonders, reconciliation, and human flourishing.

Welcome Culture as a Conversation Partner

Sadly, evangelicals as often seen as fearing culture and cultural change. We treat culture as the enemy and act out of fear and defensiveness.

Let's stop treating the culture as our enemy. Culture is our counterpoint, mirror, conversation partner, protagonist, foil, enricher, and more. We must be socially and culturally engaged since we're always culturally located. Being culturally engaged and located doesn't mean being socially and culturally reduced. Instead, we explore where society, culture, and theology have enriched, shaped, and shackled each other. Sometimes all these things are happening at once.

Evangelicals need to enter creative conversation with a wide range of disciplines. This is a two-way conversation. These disciplines include ethics, politics, philosophy, cultural studies, sociology, social theories, postcolonialism, gender and racial studies, cultural intelligence, aesthetics, creative arts, ecology, health, education, business and leadership studies, history, and more. The best kind of evangelical life see Scripture as its highest authority, but also explores how God is speaking to his church and his world through culture and a wide range of disciplines.

Seek Discipleship in Community

Evangelicals care about personal conversion. But often our discipleship is too individualistic.

Discipleship happens in community. Community is essential for changed hearts and churches. Churches must seek orthodoxy (renewed beliefs), orthopraxis (transformed practices), and orthokardia (renovated hearts). All three need to be dynamic, transforming, life-giving, and integrated. All three are about personal and corporate transformation.

The best kind of evangelical life refuses beliefs that are imposed and abstract. It rejects practices that are pragmatic and culturally reduced. And it denies spiritualities that are consumeristic and gnostic and individualistic. We need a different approach to discipleship. Jesus calls us to discover discipleship in community. God calls us into fellowship with fellow Christians, the gospel, and his sufferings, consolations, and hope. We share this vital fellowship with the Trinity, and with all God's people. A common possession unites Christians. This possession is the divine life and grace offered us in the life, death, resurrection, and hope of Jesus Christ. We become disciples together-not individually or alone.

What kind of discipleship do we need? We can't just focus on right belief or good behavior. If our goal is transformation and renewal, then we must strive after discipleship that is integrated, holistic, interdependent, missional, disciplined, renovating, revitalizing, prayerful, desirous, loving, gracious, hope-filled, and communal. This kind of discipleship only happens in community-and specifically in communities that join with God in his mission to love and restore and redeem the world.

Listen and Learn From Many Voices

Lesslie Newbigin writes, "We need the witness of Christians of other cultures to correct our culturally conditioned understanding of Scripture." It's as true to say that we need the witness of Christians of other cultures, races, denominations, and genders to correct our culturally conditioned understanding of the gospel, the Bible, mission, discipleship, community, and much more.

Sometimes evangelicals are viewed as arrogant. For some, evangelicals appear to believe that they're always right and that they have nothing to learn from others.

It's time to change that. We need to be open to the interpretations, lives, cultures, traditions, and views of others. This is about discerning God's divine presence in community and conversation and church and world. This involves humility, listening, relationship, and prayer.

A worthwhile evangelical life happens when we're attentive to (and in conversation with) church and world. We pay attention to what God is saying to us through his church by listening to traditions, interpretations, cultures, ecumenical dialogue, World Christianity, global and local theologies, and "the least of these." We notice what God is saying to us in the world by listening to philosophy, science, religions, cultures, worldviews, and more. God isn't in all these things at all times. But he's often trying to speak to us in those places.

A life of discipleship is a life of humility and learning and embrace and openness. Attentiveness is required for such faith. So, we need a new kind of open, generous evangelicalism. This evangelicalism is open to learning from other church and theological traditions, and it looks for God's work in the world.

A worthwhile, generous, broad evangelicalism grows out of conversation with many voices-including Euro-American, Majority World (Third World), Indigenous, First Nations, and diaspora (immigrant) voices.

Unite Spirit, Word, and Justice

Why are so many evangelical nervous about the work of the Spirit, and also about social justice? We need an evangelicalism that unites Spirit and Word and justice.

In Matthew 22:23–33, Jesus is engaging the Sadducees in a debate about marriage at the resurrection. He hits these religious leaders hard with these words: "You are in error because you don't know the Scriptures or the power of God." It's clear that Jesus thinks that these religious leaders don't even know what the Scriptures say about the resurrection, let alone the power of God to do supernatural, astonishing, world-transforming things.

Their errors of biblical interpretation and superficial, corrupted faith arise directly from the fact that they don't know the Scriptures or the power of God. Yet, Jesus knew both. In verse 33, we see that the crowds were "astonished" (amazed) when they heard him (as in Luke 9:43 and Acts 3:10). Jesus had the ability to amaze with his words as easily as with his signs and wonders - both produced the same reaction. This is because Jesus walked in the power of the Word and the Spirit. We must seek to know both too.

Living in the power of the Word and Spirit isn't just about biblical study and confidence in Scripture, or about signs and wonders and the gifts of the Spirit. Living in the life of the Word and Spirit is also about peacemaking and justice and the ministry of reconciliation. It's about fighting injustice, confronting exploitation, caring for creation, welcoming the stranger, and seeing the Spirit in art and beauty and culture and creation. It's about confronting issues of race, prejudice, discrimination, and reconciliation.

Living in the power of the Word and Spirit is about expressing the fruit of the Spirit, being generous and content, caring for the poor and broken, and loving our enemies. Living in the power of the Word and Spirit is about embracing the radical social ethics of the Sermon on the Mount and the Beatitudes. It's about being a people who live lives (together and in the world) that alert people to the universal rule and reign of God. It's about letting go of old dichotomies (Word-Spirit, sacred-secular, proclamation-social justice, and so on), and embracing the integral and integrative life of the Spirit. It's about living in a posture of discernment and attention: keeping in step with the Spirit and walking in daily dependence on his leading and presence and power.

What happens when Christians embrace Word and Spirit and justice? God is glorified, lives are transformed, mission is accomplished, community is revitalized, and the church experiences, afresh, God's empowering presence (his holy, purifying, true, emboldening, and transforming presence).

Be the Church and Stop With the Partisan Politics

God calls God's church to be a distinct people, with a distinct ethic, a distinct story, a distinct peace, a distinct community, a distinct diversity, and a distinct witness. As Stanley Hauerwas says, "The first responsibility of the church is to be the church . . . The church doesn't have a social ethic-the church is a social ethic." Put another way, "The church doesn't have a social strategy, the church is a social strategy."

As the new humanity in Jesus Christ, our life together is political.

We're not talking here about Republicans or Democrats or some other form of party politics. We're talking about the politics of the realm of God. Together, as God's new creation, we display a new and redeemed politic before a watching world.

Evangelicals are often too closely aligned with specific political parties. But no secular political party represents Christ. We should stop acting as though one is more worthy or godly than any other. Too often, we get caught up in the political concerns and spirits of our age. But, instead, we should show the world a new and redeemed politic by choosing to be the church.

We're called to be "alternative people" or "another city", who practice a distinct Christ-honoring life together, ethic, witness, and politic. The church is salt and light, a "city on a hill." The church of Jesus Christ is called to embrace a distinct social existence. This means that we reject violence, relinquish power, pursue holiness, embrace ethics, cultivate meaningful community, embrace missional presence, respect free association, and imitate the servant nature of Christ.

A faithful church abandons the reach for politics, power, influence, wealth, and prestige. Rather, it imitates the foolish weakness and scandal of the cross.

Pursue Peace in a Divided World

We're living in a divided and conflicted age. Evangelicals could contribute to this, or we could choose to be people of peace.

God calls the church to be a people of peacemaking and reconciliation. The Messiah is our peace, and he's abolished the conflicts and enmities that divide people (Eph 2:11–14). Peace and reconciliation are at the very heart of the new humanity in Christ. Jesus calls his church to express peace and unity, as a peaceable community. And he also calls his church to be peacemakers in a world characterized by misunderstanding, war, hatred, and animosity.

Jesus Christ showed us what peacemaking looks like, by living a life of nonviolence, justice, peace, reconciliation, and forgiveness. Not only did his say "blessed are the peacemakers, for they'll be called the children of God," he also showed us in his life and death what such peacemaking looks like (Mt 5:9). Love for enemies is the hallmark of discipleship. "Love your enemies and pray for those who persecute you, so that you may be children of your Father in heaven" (Mt 6:44-45).

God not only calls us to be peacemakers who love our enemies, God also gives us the ministry of reconciliation. "All this is from God, who reconciled us to himself through Christ, and has given us the ministry of reconciliation" (2 Cor 5:18). God reconciles the world to Godself through Christ. God calls us to be ambassadors of Spirit-empowered reconciliation-calling women and men to be reconciled to God and to each other. The new humanity in Christ is characterized by reconciliation, peacemaking, and love for enemies.

Restore Justice

Too often, evangelicals are seen as not really caring about justice. This can't continue, without doing terrible damage to our tradition and our churches.

Restoring justice involves educating ourselves about injustices in our neighborhood, society, and world. We must also educate ourselves about what it means to be a good and just neighbor for those exploited, on the margins, or suffering injustice.

Restoring justice involves talking openly and honestly about the issues. Talk about the injustices, deaths, discriminations, and atrocities. Talk about the lives and humanity of black and white and other people. Talk with people from right across the spectrum-black and white, old and young, poor and rich, Indigenous and non-Indigenous, and women and men.

Restoring justice involves listening to the concerns and perspectives of others, even when these seem to address issues that don't directly affect us. It involves standing up for the rights and wellbeing of others-even if their wellbeing or prosperity or flourishing seems only indirectly related to ours, and even when their wellbeing comes at our expense.

This is about walking in other people's shoes. It's about addressing contemporary and historical injustices, on behalf of others. We imitate the One who came into this world for our wellbeing-giving up his comfort, safety, power, and position. We follow the One who was wounded, bruised, rejected, and crucified for us. We imitate the One who restores justice in an unjust world.

Restoring justice also involves speaking and acting for justice. Restoring justice means addressing injustice head on. This includes addressing systemic and structural injustices. Sympathy must move to compassion, which must move to love, which must move to advocacy and action. Love without action is meaningless. Compassion without justice is hollow. Solidarity without advocacy is only half the picture.

We must not be silent in the face of poverty, exploitation, injustice, sexism, racism, misogyny, torture, hate, division, conflict, authoritarianism, etc. We must choose to speak and act, even when we know we will suffer the consequences.

This means speaking out on "Black Lives Matter", poverty, climate change, war, consumption and consumerism, health issues, nuclear weapons, the Palestine/Israel conflict, white privilege, sexism, racism, systemic and structural evils, and more.

Silence speaks volumes. When you or I choose not to act, we're, in fact, taking a form of action. We witness to Jesus and his kin-dom, in our life together, and in our risky, prophetic, and just words and actions.

Restoring justice involves prioritizing the wellbeing and human flourishing of the poor, wronged, marginalized, and disadvantaged. This only happens when we prioritize and value their agency and voice and redistribute power and resources.

Restoring justice includes eradicating violence against women in society and the church. It's about amplifying the voices and contributions of women in the church, and honoring and releasing their gifts.

Restoring justice means welcoming the stranger, the foreigner, the undocumented migrant, the refugee and asylum seeker, and the displaced.

Restoring justice is, fundamentally, about following a just God and being a just church. God hates injustice. God is just. The biblical story is one of a just and loving God reaching out to humanity to restore justice, wholeness, healing, and redemption. The church is an alternative

64

community. God calls this church to embrace, proclaim, embody, and practice restored justice. We do this by practicing a restored ethic, a restored hope, a restored community, a restored peace, a restored truth, a restored love, a restored reconciliation, and a restored justice.

Care About Creation and the Environment

The church can't join fully with God in his mission while it neglects its responsibility to God's creation. And I see no way that we can be disciples of Jesus without a passionate concern for his creation, and a desire to heal the planet he gave us.

Evangelicals who care nothing about creation are denying the gospel and denying the full biblical witness.

Sadly, too much of the church sees little connection between discipleship and mission and creation care. And much of the church has little interest in joining with God in his mission to redeem and restore the whole of creation.

Creation care is missional. It's essential to a missional church and theology. And it's crucial to discipleship. Creation care is a gospel issue. The gospel calls the church to care for the world God has given us to steward well.

The world is watching. Do we exercise loving care of the planet? Are we concerned about those made vulnerable through environmental degradation and climate change? Do we engage in ecological responsibility and innovation? Do we cultivate sustainable practices and simple lifestyle? Do we testify to Jesus Christ through our caring relationship with humans and the planet?

Our care for creation can witness to Jesus Christ, his gospel and kingdom, and his restoration of all things.

The Lausanne Movement and the World Evangelical Alliance organized the Lausanne Global Consultation on Creation Care and the Gospel in Jamaica in November 2012. After reflecting on Scripture and talking through the issues, the group wrote the following. Creation care is a "gospel issue within the lordship of Christ. Informed and inspired by our study of the scripture . . . Creation care is an issue that must be included in our response to the gospel, proclaiming and acting upon the good news of what God has done and will complete for the salvation of the world. This isn't only biblically justified, but an integral part of our mission and an expression of our worship to God for his wonderful plan of redemption through Jesus Christ."

Seek a Generous, Humble, and Loving Evangelicalism

Evangelicals are believers committed to living and proclaiming the *euangelion*: the "gospel" or "good news."

In this piece, I'm asking us to move away from a narrow, fear-based, exclusive, anxious, partisan, politicized, and combative evangelicalism, to one that is generous, inclusive, humble, and love-based. This is a true evangelicalism, and a true witness to the euangelion.

This true evangelicalism honors what evangelicals have always said they hold dear: the power of personal conversion, the supremacy and Lordship of Christ, the glory of the gospel, the authority of the Bible, and our call to go into all the world and make disciples.

And this true evangelicalism grasps and responds to a fuller gospel story, which calls us to a prophetic, alternative way in the world. What is this way in the world? We let the Bible move us into a passionate love for Jesus Christ. We tear down false divides and join God in mission. We welcome culture as a conversation partner, and look for signs of God's presence in the world. We seek discipleship in community, and live lives in contrast to the individualism and consumerism of our age. We're humble enough to listen and learn from many voices. We unite Spirit and Word and justice. We reject partisan politics and abandon the reach for politics, power, influence, wealth, and prestige. Instead, we seek to imitate the foolish weakness and scandal of the cross. We pursue peace in a divided world. We acknowledge our sins and mistakes, and out complicity in injustices, and seek to restore justice to those who have been wronged. We care about creation and the environment. We grasp the power of the whole gospel to change the whole church, whole lives, and the whole world.

In the process, we discover that this generous, humble, and loving evangelicalism is also a prophetic, compelling, and biblical faith.

If these twelve principles sound "evangelical," it's only because they're deeply Christian. They're not a brand to defend but a path to walk: available to every church and every pilgrim who dares to follow Jesus. Live them wherever you worship, whatever label you wear: let Scripture form you, the Spirit empower you, justice steady you, mercy soften you, and creation's groan awaken you. Let them make your life a public altar (humble, joyful, courageous) where enemies are prayed for, the vulnerable are welcomed, and truth is spoken with tears. Call them evangelical if you must, but better to call them discipleship. This is the narrow road that leads to life, for all of us, in any tradition, under one Lord.

PART III — CROSS AND RESURRECTION: HOPE AND HEALING

Part 3 explores the movement from cruciform realism to resurrection hope: where spirituality becomes public, redemptive, and embodied.

10. Cruciform: Good Friday, Global Wounds, and the Cross of Christ

Easter Friday isn't soft. It doesn't soothe or explain. It doesn't offer closure. It exposes. It reveals the violence we carry and the love we can't fathom. It unmasks our illusions: that power is enough, that empire will save us, that suffering is a failure, and that God is absent in death. Good Friday says otherwise. It tells the truth about pain, hope, divine solidarity, and human brutality. It breaks the silence, not with answers, but with presence.

"Good Friday tells the truth about pain, hope, divine solidarity, and human brutality. It breaks the silence, not with answers, but with presence."

In most modern societies, we quickly move from pain to remedy, sorrow to celebration, and loss to victory. But the cross shows us another way: crucifixion and resurrection need each other. We can't speak of resurrection without letting the cross speak its terrible and wondrous truth over all humanity and creation.

The cross is the most scandalous symbol in history: not a monument of domination but of surrender, not a tool of coercion but a tree of communion.[39] The cross of Christ isn't a theological artifact. It's the shape of the Christian life, the shape of the church, our politics, our ethics, and our posture in the world. Cruciformity isn't a metaphor; it's a way of being.

"Cruciformity isn't a metaphor; it's a way of being."

---

[39] Moltmann, *The Crucified God.*

Cruciform means shaped like a cross, reflecting the self-giving love, humility, and suffering of Jesus Christ. *Cruciformity* is the process of being conformed to the cross of Christ, embodying his pattern of sacrificial love, humility, and faithfulness in every area of life: personal, communal, ethical, and political.

Today, as creation groans, technologies rise, borders burn, nationalisms threaten, and nations unravel, we return to the cross of Jesus Christ, not as spectators of ancient pain but as people being formed by its logic of love.

The Earth at the Foot of the Cross

Good Friday speaks to a world on fire. Climate change isn't a distant apocalypse. It's a crucifixion in progress: oceans rising, forests collapsing, creatures perishing, and the vulnerable suffering first and worst. It isn't just the earth that's bleeding, but people experiencing poverty.

Christ's wounds, piercings, and sufferings are all around us: they appear in rising seas, burning forests, bleaching corals, and the sufferings of the vulnerable.[40] Christ's blood is poured out for a suffering humanity and earth.

To live a cruciform life is to stand where Christ stands: on the side of the groaning, the trampled, and the ignored. At the cross, the crucified God doesn't rise above suffering but descends into it.[41] And so must we.

This means our climate action can't be sanitized. It must be sacrificial. It must bear the weight of solidarity. Cruciform care means living lightly, protesting boldly, giving generously, planting hopefully, and grieving honestly. It means loving creation not as scenery but as sacred creation. The cross of Christ doesn't offer an escape from the world. The cross offers love strong enough to stay, care for, and protect humanity and creation.

Artificial Intelligence and the Imitation of Christ

---

[40] McFague, *A New Climate for Theology.*
[41] Gutiérrez, *A Theology of Liberation.*

We're building machines in our image faster than we can shape our souls. Artificial intelligence now writes poems, renders decisions, equips militaries, and drives economies. But the deeper question isn't what AI can do. It's what we become when we forget the crucified One.

Artificial intelligence reinforces our need for performance, speed, productivity, predictability, and control. Our AI systems are our new Babels, monuments to our desire for deity and impulse toward idolatry. But the crucified Christ invites us to slow down, live in an embodied way, express our full humanity, empty ourselves, and choose presence over power.

A society shaped by speed, control, performance, monetization, objectification, robotics, and optimization isn't cruciform. It's efficient but not compassionate. It's intelligent but not wise. The cross calls us back to the vulnerable center: to the Christ who chose powerlessness and who emptied, embodied, incarnated, suffered, and refused to dominate.

In an AI age, cruciform discipleship means slowing down, staying embodied, choosing relationship over automation, and mystery over mastery. It means using tools to serve, not to exploit. It means building systems that remember the dignity of the least and the sacredness of limits. Cruciformity doesn't fear the future and won't bow to the gods of efficiency.

The Cross at the Border

Immigration is more than politics. It's theology. When bodies move across borders, the church must remember the story of a displaced Savior. Born into state violence, hunted by the empire, Jesus fled across borders before he ever preached a sermon. The cross began with exile. The crucifixion continues whenever we build walls to keep love out and fear in.

To follow the crucified Christ is to be pierced by the grief of migrants, to be wounded by the stories that don't make headlines. It's to live with a bias toward the stranger, build tables, not walls, and defend the dignity of those the world deems disposable.

71

Cruciform hospitality isn't safe. It stretches comfort. It risks misunderstanding. But it's holy. It says: You're not illegal. You're not disposable. You're not unwanted. You're beloved. Your wounds are our wounds. And this land, this church, and this hope are big enough for you too.

Dying States, Living Christ

The world is weary. Governments crumble. Trust erodes. Violence feels closer each day. Some nations are failing in silence. Others implode on screens. The temptation is either despair or distance. But the cross of Christ does neither.

The cross enters the ruins. It doesn't deny collapse but transforms it. Cruciform faith doesn't require stability to love. It requires presence. It requires a willingness to live among the broken as people shaped by resurrection hope.

"The cross doesn't offer escape but companionship in the ruins."

When states fail, governments collapse, militaries and militias oppress, and nations fracture, the cross of Christ compels us to enter with love, truth, and hope. The cross doesn't offer escape but companionship in the ruins.

In places of political decay, the church mustn't echo the empire. It must echo the crucified. It must be a community of wounded healers, fierce compassion, and stubborn peace. The cruciform presence holds space for lament, works for justice and refuses to abandon those abandoned by systems.

The Idol of Nation

Nationalism promises belonging through exclusion, safety through suspicion, purity through walls, and glory through myth. But cruciform faith bears witness to a different allegiance. At the foot of the cross, there are no flags. There are only wounds. The cross of Christ breaks the back of tribal pride. It undoes the illusion that any nation can carry the kingdom of God.

"At the foot of the cross, there are no flags. There are only wounds."

The cross challenges and disrupts every anthem of supremacy, every symbol of exceptionalism, and every notion of political purity. The crucified Christ reminds us that God's kingdom doesn't arrive with flags but wounds.[42]

The crucified Christ isn't the mascot of an empire. Christ is the stranger, the outsider, and the one crucified by both religion and state. When the church baptizes nationalism, it ceases to be church. Cruciform discipleship means resisting every ideology that demands our worship. It means loving a place but refusing to weaponize it. It means telling the truth about history and choosing solidarity over supremacy.

The cross calls us out of self-preservation and into self-giving love: for neighbors and enemies alike. And in that love, the lie of national idolatry loses its grip.

The Interior Cross

Cruciformity isn't just a public ethic. It's an inner formation. It's the daily choice to let go of ego, empty the self, forgive the unforgivable, and carry what no one sees.[43] It's to follow Jesus not just into Galilee but into Gethsemane.

We want to see change in the world. Our temptation is always to look outside ourselves before changing within. But cruciform faith doesn't just reshape the world; it transforms us from the inside out, one prayer, one surrendered moment and one commitment to imitating the crucified Christ at a time.

Good Friday tells us that transformation rarely looks like success. It looks like surrender, dying to the need to win, and refusing to mirror the world's cruelty, even when wounded by it.

---

[42] Hauerwas, *War and the American Difference.*
[43] Gorman, *Cruciformity.*

Cruciform spirituality creates people who love without condition, suffer without becoming bitter, and serve without applause. These are the ones who carry the cross not as an ornament but as orientation.

The Mystery We Carry

We don't explain the cross. We carry it. We're shaped by it. Through it, we learn the paradox at the heart of the gospel: that weakness is strength, loss is gain, and death is the beginning of life.

We don't master the cross. We inhabit its mystery, carry its weight, and surrender to the love of Jesus Christ offered through his sacrifice.

Good Friday isn't the end. But it's the truth we must pass through to live the resurrection honestly. A Christianity without the cross is a performance. A Christianity shaped by the cross is presence: wounded, watching, waiting, and loving.

"We don't master the cross. We inhabit its mystery, carry its weight, and surrender to the love of Jesus Christ offered through his sacrifice."

So we walk with the crucified One into a world unraveling. We don't walk with fear. We walk with love.

And this love, shaped like a cross, still has the power to hold the world together.

11. Resurrection in the Ruins: Easter Hope and the Healing of the World

Resurrection Sunday isn't a retreat into denial. It isn't the triumph of optimism or the victory of spiritual escapism. It's the announcement of something unspeakably tender and radically disruptive: love has risen from the grave. Life has emerged from death. A wounded body walks again, not to erase the scars but to transfigure them.

"Resurrection doesn't ignore the world's pain; it walks right into it, still bearing the marks."

This isn't a metaphor. It's the deepest reality. The resurrection of Jesus Christ was literal, bodily, and historical.[44] Resurrection doesn't ignore the world's pain; it walks right into it, still bearing the marks. And because of this, resurrection isn't just something to believe. It's something to embody. Resurrection is a way of seeing, a way of standing, a way of loving.

We live in an age of many cruciform wounds: climate change, artificial intelligence, immigration crises, rising nationalisms, and failing states. And yet, we proclaim that resurrection still rises: not in abstraction but in resistance, new beginnings, and the remaking of all things.

The Earth Shall Rejoice

Creation groans, and resurrection answers: not with quick fixes but with renewal from within. The Risen Christ isn't disembodied light. Christ

---

[44] See Luke 24:36–43; Romans 10:9; 1 Corinthians 15:3–8; Wright, *The Resurrection of the Son of God*.

walks through gardens, eats fish, breathes on friends, laughs, and weeps. Resurrection is earthy. It affirms soil, skin, and sky.

The same power that raised Christ is now at work in creation, not to abandon it but to redeem it.[45] The resurrection calls us to live as gardeners in a burning world: to plant, compost, clean, protest, and protect. This isn't sentimental ecology. It's holy resistance and God-given stewardship.

"The resurrection calls us to live as gardeners in a burning world: to plant, compost, clean, protest, and protect."

Easter people are resurrection people. And resurrection people don't shrug at melting glaciers, disappearing species, or poisoned rivers. They grieve and act. They mourn and sow. They walk with the wounded Earth as if it matters because it does.

Machines Can't Resurrect

We're raising machines without raising our souls. Artificial intelligence expands, evolves, and encroaches. But resurrection reminds us that life isn't code; it's a gift.[46]

Easter speaks differently in the face of algorithmic control and digital domination. It says presence matters more than precision, flesh matters more than function, and mystery matters more than mastery.

The risen Christ doesn't return as an optimized spirit. Christ returns in a body that still carries trauma. This is the scandal of Christian hope: that real life is slow, sacred, and vulnerable. So, while the world marvels at machine learning, resurrection calls us to soul learning. To become wise, not just smart. Loving, not just efficient. Alive, not just animated.

"The risen Christ doesn't return as an optimized spirit. Christ returns in a body that still carries trauma."

---

[45] Moltmann, *God in Creation.*
[46] Lennox, *2084: Artificial Intelligence and the Future of Humanity.*

Cruciform spirituality embraces technology as a tool, not a master. Resurrection spirituality insists that the most human things (prayer, slowness, compassion, touch) aren't obsolete. They're eternal.

Resurrection Has No Borders

No gate was needed on Easter morning, and no tomb was guarded enough. The stone rolled back, and with it, every barrier we thought was permanent. The resurrection undoes the logic of exclusion. Resurrection dismantles walls, borders, and divisions.

Christ emerges not into a homeland but into a world. And Christ goes first to the margins: to grieving women, fearful disciples, and doubting friends. This is a migrant gospel of movement, displacement, and hospitality.

"Easter isn't a private inheritance. It's a shared homeland."

To live resurrection is to welcome the stranger as sacred.[47] Not because it's politically expedient but because it's what the Risen Christ does. Resurrection people open doors. They sit with the undocumented. They grieve deportations. They tear down the idea that any human is illegal.

Easter isn't a private inheritance. It's a shared homeland. Resurrection remakes us into one new humanity: borderless, beloved, and bearing witness to a love that moves across every line we draw.

The Empire Can't Hold

On Friday, it looked like the Roman Empire had won. Power had spoken, and the cross was its verdict. But Sunday shattered that illusion. Resurrection is the rejection of death-dealing systems.

Today's empires are subtler. Nationalism is cloaked in nostalgia. Propaganda is disguised as prayer. Glory is draped in flags. Worship is confused with politics. But resurrection refuses to salute what crucifies.

---

47 Pohl, *Making Room.*

Easter people love their lands without worshiping them. They remember that the tomb was in a garden, not a capital, and that Christ's risen body spoke peace, not dominance.

Resurrection disrupts tribal pride and calls forth a new kind of nation: not one of borders and blood, but of beatitudes and broken bread. It's a people shaped by grace, not genealogy. By cruciform love, not coercive power. But the inclusive resurrection, not ethnicity or blood.

To follow the Risen Christ is to refuse every nationalism that demands your worship. It's to pledge allegiance to the kingdom with no flag, only a cross, and now an empty tomb. All nations and empires will bow before the almighty, sovereign God and the Risen Christ, who rules and reigns in justice, righteousness, peace, and love.

Resurrection in Ruined States

When systems collapse, governments fail, trust corrodes, and cities fall, resurrection isn't absent. It begins again in the rubble.

The risen Christ didn't return to Caesar's throne. Christ returned to wounded disciples, hiding in locked rooms, clinging to scraps of hope. This is where resurrection still begins.

In failing states, resurrection moves through local churches, feeding children, planting gardens, and holding vigils. It whispers in the courage of communities that refuse to leave one another. It shows up not in spectacle but in solidarity.

Resurrection doesn't fix everything. But it makes everything possible again. It breathes into the bones of places that thought their song was over. And somehow, impossibly, the music begins again.

The Risen Christ Within

Resurrection isn't only a literal, historical, bodily event. Resurrection is an indwelling. The same Spirit that raised Christ from the dead now lives within.[48] The tomb was outside us. The life is now within us.

This means resurrection isn't a memory to admire but a force to embody. It moves us to forgive when bitterness feels justified, to rejoice when grief is still fresh, and to speak life when the world only mutters despair.

"To live resurrected is to carry a light that doesn't deny the darkness but refuses to be overcome."

The mystical path has always known this: resurrection isn't flashy. It's hidden. It's slow. It happens in the ordinary rooms of our days: as we make meals, tend wounds, tell the truth, and keep going.

To live resurrected is to carry a light that doesn't deny the darkness but refuses to be overcome.

Resurrection Is Rising

Easter isn't a weekend. It's a way. A reorientation. A revolution of how we see and live. Resurrection doesn't mean the cross didn't matter. It means the cross wasn't the end.

The same world that crucified still groans. But it's now pierced by glory. And in every place where death once reigned, something new is already breaking through.

So rise, not with denial, but with defiance. Rise with joy that is fierce. Rise with peace that disturbs. Rise with a love that bears scars and still sings. Rise with the presence of the risen Jesus Christ.

Resurrection has begun. And you, beloved, are part of it.

---

[48] See Romans 8:11. See also Willard, *Renovation of the Heart*.

Epilogue: The Sacred in the Ordinary

The city still hums. The lights flicker, the trains sigh, the endless scroll continues. Nothing seems to have changed, and yet, for those who have learned to see, everything is different. The same streets now shimmer with sacrament. The same faces once overlooked now reveal the image of God. The same noise, once deafening, has become a strange kind of liturgy: a chorus of longing rising from the pavement toward heaven.

Grace doesn't always appear in thunder. More often, it comes barely seen, like light glancing off a window, like a kindness exchanged between strangers, like a moment of stillness on a crowded bus. The kingdom of God isn't a future utopia waiting beyond history; it's a subtle revolution already unfolding within it. Every act of mercy, every breath of prayer, every small refusal to surrender to cynicism becomes part of this divine conspiracy of love.

We were never meant to escape the world. We were meant to inhabit it differently: to live with a depth the culture has forgotten, to walk slowly enough to see burning bushes beside commuter trains and Christ's face in the tired eyes of commuters. The task isn't to flee Babylon, but to sing the Lord's song within it. The gospel calls us not out of the city, but deeper into it: with open eyes, unarmored hearts, and the courage to love what is wounded.

Prophetic imagination begins in attentiveness. Before we can speak, we must learn to see. Before we confront the powers, we must be captured again by beauty. God's presence is manifest in the ordinary: laughter over dinner, tears on the curb, the smell of rain, the steady pulse of compassion that refuses to die. Every ordinary moment holds a secret invitation: *Be still. Pay attention. The Holy is here.*

This is how renewal begins: not with grand programs or strategies, but with people learning again to notice, to pray, to bless. To resist the seduction of speed. To listen longer than they speak. To choose wonder over cynicism, gratitude over complaint, solidarity over suspicion. This is the way the Spirit remakes the world: from the inside out, through those who live alert to divine presence and alive to the cries of their neighbors.

The prophets never promised an easy future. They taught us to hope anyway: to hope as resistance, as faithfulness, as defiance. Hope that plants gardens in the ruins, hope that keeps watch through the night, hope that sings when nothing seems worth singing for. Such hope isn't naïve. It's resurrection-shaped. It bears the wounds of Friday and the fire of Sunday morning.

So as you close these pages, step outside. Feel the wind on your face. Listen for the heartbeat beneath the noise. You are walking through holy ground. The Spirit still hovers over this restless city, brooding over chaos, whispering creation into being.

The sacred isn't elsewhere. It's here:
in this breath,
this street,
this moment,
this love.

Bibliography

Anonymous. *The Cloud of Unknowing*. Translated by Carmen Acevedo Butcher. Boston: Shambhala, 2009.

Brother Lawrence. *The Practice of the Presence of God*. Translated by John J. Delaney. New York: Image, 1977.

Brown Taylor, Barbara. *An Altar in the World: A Geography of Faith*. New York: HarperOne, 2009.

Gorman, Michael J. *Cruciformity: Paul's Narrative Spirituality of the Cross*. Grand Rapids: Eerdmans, 2001.

Gutiérrez, Gustavo. *A Theology of Liberation: History, Politics, and Salvation*. Translated by Sister Caridad Inda and John Eagleson. Maryknoll: Orbis, 1988.

Hauerwas, Stanley. *War and the American Difference: Theological Reflections on Violence and National Identity*. Grand Rapids: Baker Academic, 2011.

Hunter, James Davison. *To Change the World: The Irony, Tragedy, and Possibility of Christianity in the Late Modern World*. New York: Oxford University Press, 2010.

Ignatius of Loyola. *The Spiritual Exercises of Saint Ignatius*. Translated by Louis J. Puhl. Chicago: Loyola, 1951.

Jacobs, Alan. *Breaking Bread with the Dead: A Reader's Guide to a More Tranquil Mind*. New York: Penguin, 2020.

Jennings Brown, "How 'Doomscrolling' Can Be Addictive: and What You Can Do to Stop," *National Geographic*, November 10, 2020.

John of the Cross. *The Dark Night of the Soul*. Translated by E. Allison Peers. New York: Image, 1959.

John of the Cross. *The Dark Night of the Soul*. Translated by Mirabai Starr. New York: Riverhead, 2002.

Kendall, R.T. *Word and Spirit: Truth, Power, and the Next Great Move of God.* Lake Mary: Charisma House, 2019.

Lennox, John. *2084: Artificial Intelligence and the Future of Humanity.* Grand Rapids: Zondervan, 2020.

Main, John. *Word into Silence.* New York: Paulist, 1980.

McFague, Sallie. *A New Climate for Theology: God, the World, and Global Warming.* Minneapolis: Fortress, 2008.

Merton, Thomas. *The Wisdom of the Desert: Sayings from the Desert Fathers of the Fourth Century.* New York: New Directions, 1960.

Moltmann, Jürgen. *God in Creation: An Ecological Doctrine of Creation.* Minneapolis: Fortress, 1993.

Moltmann, Jürgen. *The Crucified God: The Cross of Christ as the Foundation and Criticism of Christian Theology.* Translated by R.A. Wilson and John Bowden. Minneapolis: Fortress, 1993.

Newport, Cal. *Digital Minimalism: Choosing a Focused Life in a Noisy World.* New York: Portfolio, 2019.

Nouwen, Henri J.M. *The Way of the Heart.* New York: Ballantine, 1981.

Nouwen, Henri J.M. *Making All Things New: An Invitation to the Spiritual Life.* New York: Harper & Row, 1981.

Pohl, Christine D. *Making Room: Recovering Hospitality as a Christian Tradition.* Grand Rapids: Eerdmans, 1999.

Schroder, Nina and Janet B. Wertz, "COVID-19 and Doomscrolling: The Psychological Impacts of Exposure to Distressing Online Content," *Journal of Health Psychology* 27, no. 6 (2022): 1256–64.

Smith, James K. A. *You Are What You Love: The Spiritual Power of Habit.* Grand Rapids: Brazos, 2016.

Starr, Mirabai, trans. *The Interior Castle* by Teresa of Ávila. New York: Riverhead, 2003.

Taylor, Charles. *A Secular Age.* Cambridge: Belknap Press of Harvard University Press, 2007.

Teresa of Ávila. *The Interior Castle.* Translated by E. Allison Peers. New York: Dover, 2007.

Ward, Benedicta, trans. *The Sayings of the Desert Fathers: The Alphabetical Collection*. Kalamazoo: Cistercian, 1984.

Willard, Dallas. *Renovation of the Heart: Putting on the Character of Christ*. Colorado Springs: NavPress, 2002.

Wright, N.T. *The Resurrection of the Son of God*. Minneapolis: Fortress, 2003.

Appendix 1: Discussion Guide

Secular City, Sacred Soul

1. Where do you most feel God's absence in your daily life, and what might it mean to seek God's presence there rather than flee from it?
2. The text says, "The city isn't godless; it's often just distracted." What kinds of distractions most numb our awareness of the holy?
3. What practices help you cultivate attentiveness and stillness amid the noise of modern life?
4. How can "monks of the metro" become a living witness to God's grace in workplaces, cafés, and streets?
5. What might change in your neighborhood or vocation if you began to treat ordinary moments as potential sacraments?

The Decline of Religion or the Dark Night of the West?

1. The chapter suggests the decline of religion may be a purification rather than a collapse. Do you see evidence of this refining in contemporary faith?
2. How does the "dark night" metaphor help us interpret cultural despair and spiritual fatigue in the West?
3. When have you experienced a personal season that felt like divine absence? What hidden grace emerged from it?
4. What idols (comfort, certainty, control) might God be stripping away from the modern church?

5. How can communities of faith embody hope without nostalgia when the structures of Christendom fall away?

Lonely But Not Alone

1. What forms of loneliness do you encounter most often in your context: social, emotional, or spiritual?
2. The chapter distinguishes loneliness from solitude. How might reclaiming solitude as "the presence of God" transform your inner life?
3. Which contemplative practices (breath prayer, silence, examen, creation care) could help you befriend your loneliness rather than fear it?
4. In what ways can solitude deepen (not diminish) our capacity for community and compassion?
5. How can the church respond prophetically and pastorally to the loneliness epidemic without offering quick fixes?

Doomscrolling and Pseudo-Transcendence

1. The chapter describes doomscrolling as "a liturgy in disguise." In what ways do our daily digital habits shape us spiritually: what do they teach us to love, fear, and desire?
2. "We become what we behold. The gaze forms the soul." What are you beholding most often? How does that shape your emotions, prayer life, and ability to be present?
3. The text contrasts doomscrolling with prayerful attention. What practices could help you reclaim your attention as an act of love rather than compulsion?
4. How might communities of faith model "holy attention" in an attention economy that profits from distraction and outrage?
5. The piece says, "Our fingers flick the screen, but our hearts long to touch eternity." Where do you sense that longing in yourself or your culture, and how might God be inviting you to meet it differently?

TikTok, Temptations, and Teresa's Interior Castle

1. What parallels do you see between Teresa's "interior castle" and the modern soul's struggle for attention in digital culture?
2. How does your engagement with technology shape your spiritual hunger, for better or worse?
3. Which "rooms" of your own interior life might God be inviting you to revisit or reclaim from distraction?
4. What daily rhythms or "digital fasts" could help you cultivate presence, depth, and peace?
5. How can contemplative stillness become a form of resistance to the algorithms of hurry, performance, and self-curation?

Critical Theory and the Cloud of Unknowing

1. How might "holy unknowing" reshape the way we approach divisive conversations about justice, gender, or race?
2. The chapter warns that certainty can become a kind of idolatry. Where might this be true in your own spiritual or theological formation?
3. What would it look like for you to practice "sacred listening as resistance" in polarized spaces: both online and in person?
4. How can we hold together truth and humility so that our speech heals rather than wounds?
5. What disciplines could help you enter the "cloud between us" and find God's presence amid disagreement and discomfort?

The Sacred Gift of Free Speech

1. "Words create worlds." Where have you seen speech heal or harm within your family, church, or nation?
2. How can Christians defend free speech while ensuring that our words remain rooted in truth and love?
3. What spiritual disciplines might help you speak less reactively and more redemptively in public life?

4. How do Jesus's examples of both bold speech and holy silence inform your own use of language?

5. What would it mean for your community to model "holy speech" in a culture addicted to outrage?

Four Ways to Live in the Power of the Spirit and the Word

1. Where in your life or church do you see imbalance: Word without Spirit, or Spirit without Word?

2. How can Scripture study and charismatic experience enrich rather than oppose each other?

3. What does humility look like when bridging divides between different theological traditions?

4. How can living "in the power of the Word and Spirit" transform social action and justice work?

5. What concrete practice this week could help you integrate truth and power, Scripture and presence?

Twelve Ways to Follow Jesus in a Secular Age

1. Which of the twelve practices speaks most powerfully to your own discipleship in today's world?

2. How can we recover a generous, humble evangelicalism that embodies both gospel conviction and social compassion?

3. What might it look like for your community to unite proclamation, justice, creation care, and reconciliation?

4. How does following Jesus in a secular age require both courage and gentleness?

5. In what ways can your everyday vocation (work, art, parenting, politics) become a site of faithful presence and witness?

Cruciform

1. The chapter claims that "cruciformity isn't a metaphor; it's a way of being." What does that mean for your discipleship?

2. How does the cross expose the idols of nationalism, consumerism, and technological control in today's world?

3. In what ways might a cruciform faith shape our responses to ecological crisis, migration, and political collapse?

4. What does it mean for you personally to "stand where Christ stands": among the wounded and those experiencing poverty?

5. How can churches cultivate cruciform love that confronts injustice without becoming bitter or violent?

Resurrection in the Ruins

1. "Resurrection doesn't ignore the world's pain; it walks right into it." How does this vision challenge sentimental or triumphalist faith?

2. Where do you see signs of resurrection in the ruins of your community or nation?

3. How might resurrection hope inform how you engage issues like climate change, migration, or political polarization?

4. The risen Christ still bore wounds. What does that reveal about the healing God offers?

5. How can resurrection people embody joy and defiant love without denying suffering?

Appendix 2: Would You Help?

Writing a book takes immense effort. It's a sustained labor of love over months, even years. Every page carries hours of thought, prayer, revision, and hope. And while the writing may be solitary, the life of a book is communal. That's where you come in. If this book has meant something to you, I'd be deeply grateful if you could help it find its way into more hands and hearts.

There are two simple but powerful ways you can do that.

First, consider leaving a short review on Amazon (and Goodreads would be wonderful too). Even just a few sentences can help others discover the book, as reviews significantly influence how books are recommended and shared online. You can do that by visiting Amazon or searching for this book and writing a review. Even a short note helps people find the book.

Second, if the book has stirred something in you, would you share it with others: friends, groups, churches, or anyone who might benefit from its message?

Your support helps keep this work going, and it means more than I can say. Thank you for being part of this journey.

Find this book on these pages:
1. Amazon:
https://www.amazon.com.au/stores/author/B008NI4ORQ
2. Goodreads:
https://www.goodreads.com/author/show/20347171.Graham_Joseph
_Hill
3. Author Website:

https://grahamjosephhill.com/books/

Appendix 3: About Me

Graham Joseph Hill (OAM, PhD) is an Adjunct Research Fellow and Associate Professor at Charles Sturt University, and one of Australia's most prolific and awarded Christian authors. He's written more than twenty books, including *Salt, Light, and a City*, which was named Jesus Creed's 2012 Book of the Year (church category); *Healing Our Broken Humanity* (with Grace Ji-Sun Kim), named Outreach Magazine's 2019 Resource of the Year (culture category); and *World Christianity*, shortlisted for the 2025 Australian Christian Book of the Year. In 2024, Graham was awarded the Medal of the Order of Australia (OAM) for his service to theological education. He lives in Sydney with his wife, Shyn.

Author and Ministry Websites

GrahamJosephHill.com
GrahamJosephHill.Substack.com
youtube.com/@GrahamJosephHill_Author
Linktr.ee/dailydevotions
facebook.com/grahamjosephhill/
instagram.com/grahamjosephhill/
amazon.com.au/stores/author/B008NI4ORQ
goodreads.com/author/show/20347171.Graham_Joseph_Hill

Books

See all my books at GrahamJosephHill.com/books

Appendix 4: Connect With Me

I'd love to stay connected with you. You can sign up to my Substack, Spirituality and Society with Hilly, where I share new writing, spiritual reflections, and updates on future books. Please find me on Substack: https://grahamjosephhill.substack.com

You can also find my books on my website: https://grahamjosephhill.com/books

You can also connect with me through my Facebook author page: https://www.facebook.com/GrahamJosephHill/

www.ingramcontent.com/pod-product-compliance
Lightning Source LLC
Chambersburg PA
CBHW020512030426

42337CB00011B/344